MERCHANT PRINCE

The Story of Alexander Duncan McRae

Betty O'Keefe and Ian Macdonald

Heritage
House

Copyright © 2001 Betty O'Keefe and Ian Macdonald

National Library of Canada Cataloguing in Publication Data

O'Keefe, Betty, 1930-
  Merchant Prince

  Includes index.
  ISBN 1-894384-30-X

  1. McRae, Alexander Duncan, 1874-1946. 2. Businessmen—
British Columbia—Vancouver—Biography. 3. Vancouver (B.C.)—
Biography. 4. Canada, Western—History. I. Macdonald, Ian, 1928–
II. Title.

FC3826.1.M37O33 2001   971.1'3303'092   C2001-911232-7
F1089.5.V22O33 2001

First edition 2001

Heritage House acknowledges the financial support for our
publishing program from the Government of Canada through the
Book Publishing Industry Development Program (BPIDP), Canada
Council for the Arts, and the British Columbia Arts Council.

Cover and book design by Darlene Nickull
Edited by Terri Elderton

HERITAGE HOUSE PUBLISHING COMPANY LTD.
Unit #108 - 17665 66 A Ave., Surrey, B.C. V3S 2A7

Printed in Canada

BRITISH
COLUMBIA
ARTS COUNCIL
We acknowledge the support of the Province of British Columbia
through the British Columbia Arts Council

The Canada Council | Le Conseil des Arts
for the Arts | du Canada

Dedication

This book is dedicated with affection to our own grandchildren, a new generation of young Canadians: Adam, Tom, and Colleen Woodward; Daniel, Charlotte, and Erin Gadsby; Elizabeth and Edward Ross; and Kayla and Matthew Macdonald.

Acknowledgements
and Special Thanks

In particular the authors want to thank the two remaining granddaughters of Alexander Duncan McRae—Jocelyn Roche of London, England and Audrey Wittner of Airdrie, Alberta—for their comments and recollections about their grandfather, a man who significantly influenced their early years and a man they both recalled with deep affection.

Without the assistance of the University Women's Club and access to their archives and photo library, this book would never have been started, nor completed. The co-operation and suggestions provided by members of the Archives Committee were greatly appreciated.

The authors would also like to thank many others for their generous assistance in providing information about Alexander Duncan McRae, from his birth to his considerable achievements in many regions of Canada and in Minnesota. We are very grateful to those who helped us in researching the details we sought about this remarkable man and his fascinating life: Helen Abbott, Vancouver; Diana Bellhouse, University Women's Club, Vancouver; John Boultbee, McRae family friend in Vancouver; John Bovey, archivist, Victoria and Winnipeg; Barbara Collett, McRae family friend, Vancouver; Reverend George Hamilton, Middlesex County Historical Society, Glencoe, Ontario; Naomi Hopkins, McRae family friend, Vancouver; Elizabeth Kelly, Duluth Public Library, Minnesota; Edith Lockwood, McRae relative,

Glencoe, Ontario; Vera Lucas, Victoria; Joy McCusker, McRae family friend, Vancouver; Sheena Macdonald, Vancouver; Bev New, archivist, University Women's Club; Sue Richardson, parliamentary assistant, Ottawa; Jim Storey, Qualicum Beach Historical and Museum Society; Walter Vanderkwaak, Glencoe Transcript and Free Press, Ontario; Fanta Verchere, McRae family friend, West Vancouver; Pat Wallace, former *Province* Women's Page Editor, West Vancouver; Mary Warner, Morrison County Historical Society, Little Falls, Minnesota; Leisl Westfall, Coquitlam Heritage Society; and Ian Woodward, arborist, Bowen Island.

This biography is based on archival materials and personal interviews, and is accurate according to available information. In some cases the authors made logical assumptions or took the occasional literary liberty.

Contents

Prologue

According to novelist Ayn Rand, and more recently Edwin Locke in his book entitled *The Prime Movers—Traits of the Great Wealth Creators*, successful men and women possess seven traits that give them the ability to become fabulous creators of wealth.

In the latter half of the nineteenth century several men born in the small rural community of Glencoe, Ontario possessed these qualities, and together they had a significant impact on the development of Canada in the first half of the twentieth century.

The seven traits necessary to achieve the kind of fame and fortune realized by these Glencoe men, according to Rand and Locke, and listed in order of importance are the following:

- **Independent Vision** or the ability to see the potential in the development of a product, service, technology, or market;
- **An Active Mind** that is impatient, constantly asks questions, and challenges assumptions;
- **Competence and confidence** in the areas where their vision takes them;
- **A drive to action** because of an impatient mind that seems to work faster than others because it knows what actions are important;
- **Egoistic passion** that amounts to a profoundly personal, selfish love of work and the rewards that come with success;

- **Love of ability** in others or the need to hire and develop outstanding people who know more about some aspects of the business than does the person with independent vision; and
- **Virtue,** because these people are motivated by traits considered virtuous such as rationality, independence, productivity, honesty, integrity, and justice.

The neighbours from Glencoe possessed all these traits, making them among "The Prime Movers" in a young Canada. Alexander Duncan McRae was the youngest of the group from Glencoe and Andrew Duncan Davidson—twenty years his senior— was the oldest. Davidson had quickly recognized the potential of the younger man, taken an early interest in his development as an entrepreneur, taught him the ways of banking, and encouraged him to study law. Alexander was encouraged to join the five already wealthy Davidson brothers in various enterprises, and together they developed creative profitable pursuits, amassed great wealth, and significantly influenced their time.

McRae's exploits ranged further afield than those of the others. He was initially involved in banking and insurance in the American mid-west and these pursuits led him into land speculation on the Canadian prairies. He then made a conscious decision to remain in Canada, and invested in the fishing, mining, and lumber industries on the Pacific Coast before he made his mark on the Canadian political scene, serving as a federal Member of Parliament (MP) and then as a senator. Finally, in his declining years, he returned to the land, developing an enormous experimental farm on 4,000 acres at Qualicum Beach on Vancouver Island. McRae remained true to the country of his birth while the Davidsons retained much stronger ties to the United States.

The life story of Alexander Duncan McRae begins on a farm in Ekfrid County, Ontario and ranges from Minnesota to Saskatchewan, to British Columbia, to England during the First World War, and finally to Ottawa. His impact on the Canadian scene, on Saskatchewan, and on B.C. in particular was significant, and it is unfortunate that his vision did not include preserving a record of his own achievements. Historians are left to dig deeply into the files of national and regional libraries to find information about the life and times of this flamboyant, likeable, and often impatient man of an era that passed into history shortly after the Second World War. Always a private man, McRae left no personal papers in safekeeping, no memoirs of his service as a major general in the First World War, no account of his recommendations to the British government, or his extensive travels in northern Canada and Alaska; if he did, they have been lost or may have been burned after he died. He was a complex and enigmatic man, known by reputation to many because of his great wealth, but perhaps truly known to very few.

McRae made his early money in the United States as did most ambitious young men of his time and while not brushing shoulders with the Vanderbilts, the Carnegies, or the Rockefellers, he was impressed by their great wealth, their opulent lifestyle, and the grandeur they created around themselves. In his own way he emulated their lifestyle. Carefully tutored by his cousin, Andrew Duncan Davidson, who already had an established reputation in banking and extensive farming interests in Minnesota, McRae acquired the energetic drive of American business pioneers, adopted their eagerness to take speculative risks, and developed the confident, unbounded ambition and insightful vision of the future he needed to become a wealthy man in his own right. McRae often took chances. He was not the cautious Canadian of repute.

His profoundly successful Canadian career began as a partner in a company organized with the Davidson brothers that bought and sold millions of acres of what was to become the province of Saskatchewan. Their description of the land as the future breadbasket of the world played a major role in encouraging colonization of the area. The men correctly envisioned the future, seeing that the American West was running short of low priced farmland, and identifying lands of the Canadian West as the new farming frontier.

11

Alexander Duncan McRae, born in Ontario, left an indelible mark on Canada in the first half of the twentieth century through his efforts in colonizing the prairies, and in building the largest lumber milling operation in British Columbia.

Throughout his life McRae found it necessary to retain close connections with American bankers and investors because little investment capital was available in Canada; his two wives were both born in the United States as were two of his daughters and three of their six husbands, but he remained a staunch Canadian. "Canada first, last and all the time," he told the House of Commons at one point during the four years he was a Member of Parliament. It was a heartfelt emotion expressed by a man who normally showed little personal emotion in public and was not a great orator.

His political career was quixotic. He played no overt role in local government or civic affairs, his vision constantly seeking broader horizons. Tired of the old-line parties in B.C. and their financial policies, he formed his own Provincial Party; but after its first disastrous election campaign, he quickly left this expensive experiment behind and turned his attention to federal politics. He won a seat as an MP, masterminded the leadership campaign for Conservative R.B. Bennett, and then organized the election strategy that made Bennett prime minister of Canada. The great irony was that McRae, too involved in the campaign at the national level, lost his own seat in the process. Despite this, he was for many years touted as a future leader of the Conservative Party, but he was more an accomplished organizer than a politician and he knew it. McRae abandoned elected politics for a Senate appointment. Throughout his public and private life he staunchly advocated rugged individualism, but spoke out in the Commons and the Senate for government aid and massive public works to provide jobs for those Canadians clearly identified as being in need.

He had great faith in the future of Canada and at one point during the Depression declared, "We are rich in citizenship. Our people have in their veins the blood

McRae and his daughters in 1906.

of the best and most progressive nations the world has ever known. We cannot be lacking in ability to see ourselves through." A nominal Presbyterian, he was a casual Christian, and his three daughters had among their six husbands a Roman Catholic and a Jew. These three, his immediate descendants, were described in the vernacular of the time as "fast" young women, spoiled princesses of the "Roaring Twenties," who were in the end, the source of considerable heartache for Vancouver's "merchant prince." He stood by each of them and then continued to lavish his love and attention on the three granddaughters who followed.

Like most Canadians of his time he favoured an end to Asian immigration and was a member of the Asiatic Exclusion League. He was also an imperialist and an admirer of much that was British. Following his outstanding service to the British government McRae and his wife were presented at court in London, England.

McRae often was described as a philanthropist, and his greatest gift was undoubtedly the donation in 1942 of Hycroft, his 30-room mansion, sold for one dollar to the federal government for use as a returned veterans' hospital. It benefited some of the men who had served in the First World War, where McRae was significantly involved, as well as for some veterans of the Second World War.

Although conservative in public life, he was often generous and flamboyant with close friends. He enjoyed the trappings of wealth and fine living and was a generous host to a wide circle of his own friends as well as his daughters' friends. To his many nieces and nephews he was fun-loving "Uncle Mac." His grandchildren adored him. To others, he filled the role of genial squire. His great wealth separated him from the common man and he lived in an "upstairs-downstairs" milieu, although he never forgot his modest beginnings. Both his household employees and the thousands who worked in his various enterprises admired his practices and policies.

McRae chose well when he selected men to run his enterprises, but he had no son nor a visionary prodigy to follow in his footsteps; so there was no dynasty, and he became all but forgotten. Alexander Duncan McRae deserves more than the fleeting references made to him in Canadian history books. His vision encompassed the future development of B.C. and Canada. In his lifetime he solved what to others would have been insurmountable challenges, battled vindictive political foes, and yet remained respected and recognized as a man of achievement for his contributions to the betterment of his colleagues and his country.

Today in Vancouver a short street bears his name: one-block long McRae Avenue. Hycroft, the stately mansion he built on the Shaughnessy hillside overlooking the city, remains the focal point of the avenue and is now home to the University Women's Club of Vancouver. On the grounds is the soaring, sequoia tree he planted almost a century ago. Both remain a part of Vancouver's heritage and are lasting memorials to Alexander Duncan McRae, B.C.'s "merchant prince."

Glencoe

The tiny settlement of Glencoe in Upper Canada took its name from a lonely glen in the western Highlands that fills a grim page in Scotland's turbulent, savage history. It was a tragic place where in 1692 visiting members of Clan Campbell, at the time in league with the English, fell treacherously on their hosts Macdonald and murdered men, women, and children. In the wars between the Scots and the English, the killing continued for many years, and in 1746 Bonnie Prince Charlie's clansmen—claymore-wielding fighters who had marched bravely but hopelessly into England before retreating in disarray—were slaughtered on the fields at Culloden. The victors under the "Butcher" Duke of Cumberland, the king's son, killed wounded Scots as they lay on the field of battle, hounded the survivors through the glens and over the mountains, and put to the sword many of those they captured. The English conquerors and their Scottish supporters then began the Highland clearances, the removal of families from their small holdings because sheep had become more important than people. Wool was needed for the mills to the south. Crofts were burned, crops destroyed, and the clans people dispersed. Starvation soon made their everyday lives starker than they had ever been before just so that large estates could be created and flocks of sheep built up.

For many there was a glimmer of hope, a way to avoid a hopeless future in Scotland: It was to leave behind the dear land, and embark on a long and dangerous journey to the new world and to the uncertainties of a strange and distant place. After much discussion and heart searching, some of the Clan McRae decided it was their only hope. Led by a priest, Alexander MacDonell Scotus, some 300 sailed away in a ship called *MacDonald*. After a hazardous, cramped voyage in primitive conditions, the men, women, and children sailed up the St. Lawrence River and landed at Quebec City in 1785. They established a settlement, a new community they called Glengary. The first McRae born in Canada, Farquhar McRae, arrived the next year. It was a different, often difficult life, but the remnants of the Clan McRae cleared the land, farmed, survived, and multiplied.

The more adventurous gradually moved farther west, some putting down roots in southwestern Ontario where they again tilled the land, went into business, and built brick homes and buildings reminiscent of Scotland, which grew into villages and small towns. The most famous McRae in Canada came from this area. He was Colonel John McRae, the surgeon-soldier, who wrote the epic poem "In Flanders Field" as he grieved the savagery of the First World War and its horrible lists of casualties. He became one of them, dying in France where poppies still bloom near his grave. In all likelihood the man in Flanders was a distant relative of the McRaes of Glencoe as there were many of them. This tiny Ontario settlement, lying 50 kilometres southwest of the city of London, became home to a whole new colony of Clan McRae. It is rolling, farm country, not at all like the bleak, narrow, mountain-hemmed glen in the Scottish Highlands after which it was named.

In the middle of the nineteenth century Alexander Duncan McRae's father and mother, Duncan Alexander McRae and Mary (Mawhinney) McRae, began farming the south half of Lot 17, Concession two, of Ekfrid Township. This branch of the McRae family did not leave Scotland until 1820 when letters from other clan members enticed them first to Quebec. Duncan McRae's older sister Christina was married to William Davidson, and they had established a farm in Glencoe some years earlier. The men here were good farmers and hard workers, living in a community where large families were common and support from relatives was readily available whenever it was needed. In fact the community was so closely knit that many family names were the same and certain popular Christian names were often repeated in different families. Duncan McRae and his new wife Mary travelled across Ontario largely by canoe before settling near the Davidsons in Ekfrid. As the years went by the two families worked side by side, helped in the fields and on their homestead by a large number of daughters and sons.

Mary McRae's mother had immigrated to Canada as a widow with three small children. During the sometimes stormy Atlantic crossing, she met a widower named Mawhinney who had three children of his own. Together they comforted the six children in their care, and shortly after their arrival in Canada, they were married. Three and three were six and in no time at all became a family with nine children. Mary McRae had no qualms about delivering a large family like her mother. She must have despaired a little, however, when her sixth daughter Sara was born, knowing how much her husband wanted a son. Her other daughters in order were Annie, Mary, Flora, Nellie, and Margaret. Finally, Alexander Duncan McRae was born on November 17, 1874, the seventh child of Duncan Alexander McRae and his wife Mary. Two more sons followed: Randolph, born a couple of years later, and William who suffered a serious fall at the age of three, which led to his death when he was only five.

The working days were long and life was not easy, but Duncan McRae and his brother-in-law William Davidson worked the land together and their families prospered. Both men were firm believers in education and insisted that all their children, girls included, complete high school. Each one in turn was enrolled in the tiny one-room Appin School. As the community grew and a larger secondary school was built, they transferred to it. While there, young Alexander learned he was not the only child in the community with the name of Alexander McRae. Alexander A. McRae, born just four years before him on January 27, 1870, was a distant cousin, and the school teacher made much of the fact that the second Alexander McRae must live up to the reputation for good marks established by the first. When not attending classes Duncan's son learned farming at his father's side, an occupation to which he would return in later life. He was paid 50 cents a day to work on the family farm. The McRaes and the Davidsons enrolled their sons at a nearby business school in Chatham, offering them the opportunity to escape farm life should they want to do so. The Davidsons had provided each of their five sons with business training before Duncan's first son graduated from high school. Alexander was also given the advantage of business school training, but that was the end of his formal education; however, it was more than the majority of farm boys in the region received.

Upon graduation Alexander McRae went to work in Duluth, Minnesota with his cousin, Andrew Davidson, who was twenty years his senior and had an established business reputation in that state. Andrew Duncan Davidson, born in Glencoe on May 18, 1853, was the eldest son of William Davidson and Christina (McRae) Davidson who had had eight children: five boys and three girls. The older two boys in the large family, Andrew and his brother Alexander—born in 1855—were the first to enter business in the United States, but were soon followed by their three younger brothers: James, Donald, and William. Both Andrew and his brother Alexander found employment initially with a railway that had branches in Wisconsin, Illinois, and Minnesota. Appointed station agent in Little Falls, which lies midway between Duluth and Minneapolis in Morrison County, Minnesota, Andrew became well-known in the community. The likeable outgoing young man was soon elected mayor. Using innovative marketing and financing techniques, he began selling railway land to homesteaders in the Midwest. Andrew also used his elected office as a stepping-stone to further his career. He become a friend of the state governor who a few years later bestowed him with the honorary title of colonel, awarded for services rendered to his community and the state of Minnesota. Andrew had provided a secure banking depository for state funds and the governor bestowed the title in recognition of this important service and as a personal thank you to the mayor of Little Falls. Following his older brother's lead, Alexander Davidson became a telegraph operator in Wisconsin, but then soon joined Andrew in business in Minnesota. It was the beginning of a dynasty.

In 1876, Andrew returned to Ontario and married Ella McRae, another member of clan McRae from his hometown, Glencoe. They returned to Duluth, which soon became the centre of the Davidson brothers' money-making enterprises. Ella McRae was not directly related to Alexander Duncan McRae, but was probably the sister of Alexander A. McRae whom Alexander Duncan had known at school.

The first banking venture for the Davidsons was in Little Falls where Andrew had established himself as a leader in the community. It opened in 1888 and a year later was recapitalized and renamed the First National Bank of Little Falls. The younger Davidsons—James, Donald, and William—soon found employment with their older brothers, and by the mid-1890s the brothers were all making good money. Andrew and Alexander Davidson were accepted throughout Minnesota as prosperous investors with a good business reputation and a growing stature in the state.

A story in *The Northwest Magazine,* which appeared in November 1892, explains some of the early successes achieved by the Davidson brothers in Minnesota and the history that led to the honorary title bestowed upon Andrew.

> Among the successful business enterprises that have come to Little Falls within the past four years there is none that the citizens of this rapidly growing young city refer to with more pride than the First National Bank. Located as it is, on one of the best business corners in the city, in a substantial and commodious brick block, the interior of their banking room is of the most modern finish and style. It is safe to say that there is not a handsomer or more conveniently arranged banking room in Minnesota. No expense has been spared in securing a strictly fire and burglar-proof vault. In it they have one of McNeale & Urban's latest improved burglar-proof steel safes weighing nearly five tons. They had also put in for the use of their customers 150 steel

safety deposit boxes for the safe keeping of papers and other valuables.

The bank was first opened as a private bank in January, 1888 by A.D. Davidson and A.R. Davidson and reorganized as a national bank on June 1, 1889, with a paid-up capital of $50,000. It has been very successful from the start; has paid an annual dividend of ten per cent and added $25,000 to its surplus. The bank is conservatively managed by men who are thoroughly familiar with banking and who are always foremost in assisting any enterprise or project that is for the best interests of Little Falls. It not only enjoys the fullest confidence of the people of Little Falls and Morrison County, but is equally well regarded throughout the state, as is shown by the fact that it has been designated as a state depository for the safe-keeping of a large portion of the money belonging to the State of Minnesota. It is also authorized depository for county and city funds.

From the outset Andrew Davidson was president and Alexander Davidson cashier of the Little Falls Bank. Before long the Davidson brothers also owned a controlling interest in the Citizens National Bank of Wahpeton, North Dakota, where Don Davidson was cashier; in the Bank of Hutchinson, in Hutchinson, Minnesota, where the youngest brother William Davidson was cashier; and in the Bank of Elbow Lake, Elbow Lake, Minnesota, where Andrew was vice-president. In the days when family honour and reputation were paramount and when business deals were sealed with a handshake, the Davidsons kept their enterprises under tight family control, although new operations were often capitalized with the help of influential local business partners.

By the time Alexander Davidson was married in Little Falls in 1892 to Laura Tanner, daughter of one of the town's most prominent citizens, the Davidsons were well-known, respected businessmen. The marriage, which linked the two well-respected families, was widely reported by newspapers in Little Falls.

In the same year, at the age of eighteen, young Alexander McRae joined the Davidsons in Duluth. Under Andrew's tutelage he began a rapid learning process that soon earned him a promotion to the now prestigious bank in Little Falls. Andrew recognized immediately that young Alexander had a wonderful way with figures and also had an ability to analyze a financial statement better and faster than men twice his age. In addition to his growing business acumen, McRae took with him to Minnesota the teachings of a strict Presbyterian household imparted by loving parents, pride in his Scottish heritage, and an ambition to prove his worth in business to all his cousins. He also had the unqualified support of the Davidsons and an easy introduction to the top bankers in the state. McRae was soon making $20 a week, so his mentor encouraged him to learn more about the business world, and to study law and industrial insurance at a local law office.

McRae was soon ready to make an investment of his own. With $1,500 provided by his father, he became a junior partner with Davidson in a company that insured grain elevators. Located at Suite 212, The Exchange Building, in Duluth, the Davidson-McRae Company sold fire and liability insurance and surety bonds. The firm prospered, and by the late 1890s the Davidson brothers and Alexander McRae had invested in a variety of new ventures. The Lumbermen's and Miners' Bank of Hibbing was owned by Andrew Davidson, Alexander McRae, and A.M. Chisholm, a prominent businessman from that community. With the addition of new capital it was soon reorganized to become the First National Bank of Hibbing; Andrew was president and Alexander McRae was vice-president. Before he was 25 years of age McRae, on his own account, had amassed $50,000 in earnings from his joint ventures.

One of the largest enterprises undertaken by the Davidsons and McRae was the purchase of a granite quarry a few miles east of Little Falls. According to newspaper accounts, the $50,000 initial capital investment was put up by president and treasurer Alexander Davidson; vice-president F. E. Kenaston; manager Andrew Davidson; and secretary Alexander McRae. Kenaston was a man who supported a number of the groups' joint ventures and later was one of the principal investors in their first Canadian undertaking, one which would prove to be phenomenally lucrative for all of them. The new quarry operation was personally managed by Alexander Davidson. His wife's position in the community ensured the market was theirs. The new owners first purchased the former Little Falls Granite Company, which provided a ready supply of black granite, and then began development of a light granite quarry to the southeast of the town. Granite was cut in large blocks and then shipped to Little Falls for further cutting and polishing. The company employed a large number of skilled stonecutters who were trained at preparing tombstones, specializing in monumental work. With the rapid influx of new people and new businesses to the area, the owners also made plans to expand into building construction as soon as possible.

Still in his mid-twenties, Alexander Duncan McRae was recognized in Minnesota as a successful young entrepreneur on his way to bigger and better things. Handsome and nearly six feet tall, he had a compact build, heavy features, and dark, penetrating eyes. His brown hair, to his sorrow, was already showing signs of thinning, but this gave him a look of maturity he would not otherwise have possessed. It was a factor which made him more acceptable to the wealthy clientele he

One of the early ventures undertaken by Andrew Davidson and Alexander McRae was advertised in 1902 by a Duluth, Minnesota city directory.

would soon approach to assist with financing for a gigantic project that had a far reaching effect on the whole of the American mid-west and the Canadian prairies.

Life wasn't all business, however; young Alexander McRae's favourite recreational pursuits included hunting and fishing, two activities he had learned at home on the farm with his father. They were well suited to his new lifestyle in Minnesota where they were also the popular pastimes of the wealthy men of the region. It was Andrew Davidson who introduced McRae to Blaunche Latimer Howe, the daughter of a wealthy mill owner who had amassed a considerable fortune in the forest industry in Pennsylvania and then multiplied his millions as a miller and investor in Minnesota. Davidson saw marriage to the young woman as an excellent match for McRae. It would give him new and influential contacts in the business and political communities and new access to men of wealth with money to invest. The young couple had many common interests, and McRae was impressed with Blaunche's sophistication, her capabilities as a hostess, her cultured voice and impeccable manners, her polished social presence, and her practiced ability as an equestrian. Blaunche was 23 years old, an attractive, well educated, enthusiastic horsewoman, and the darling of both her mother and her father. Alexander, now 26, and Blaunche were married in Minneapolis on February 23, 1900. The governor of the state and many of Minnesota's most influential citizens attended their wedding.

Minnesota was in the breadbasket of America—a land that fed a growing, hungry population. As the price of farmland in the mid-west climbed, farmers began to move farther west to find affordable acreage. It was then that the men from Glencoe identified a new opportunity for themselves. They knew that to the north in the land of their birth there was a massive stretch of prairie grassland, sparsely populated, freezing cold in winter, but capable of growing wheat, rye, flax, and other cereal crops just as well as the lands of Minnesota. They studied the potential of the Canadian prairie carefully, made several trips to the territory west of Winnipeg, and then prepared to make their move. The older

Davidson brothers, Andrew and Alexander, along with Alexander McRae, and a number of their wealthy business associates were about to invest a fortune in land that within a few years—in 1905—would become the province of Saskatchewan.

With a new wife, a healthy bank account, and an exciting new development project in mind, McRae was ready to return to the land of his birth. Together he and the Davidsons created a project of breathtaking proportions, which included settlement on a scale never seen before: a huge section of the Canadian West.

It was the vision of these men as well as their creativity and ability to raise funds, organize, and deliver a scheme of unprecedented size that made it so extremely lucrative for the original investors. Their timing was also impeccable. Land near Saskatoon sold in 1899 for $1 an acre and by 1902, when Andrew Davidson and Alexander McRae had amassed five million acres, the price was $20 per acre.

The Canadian Pacific Railway (CPR), the country-connecting line, had been built through the prairies in the 1880s, reaching the Pacific coast and heralding the arrival there of pioneer settlers. But the silent stretches of the prairies between Winnipeg and the Rocky Mountains remained sparsely populated, a vast rolling grassland in summer and a barren white wasteland in winter. At the turn of the century, the prairie west of Manitoba was included in the great sprawling area known as the North West Territories. Both the federal government and the CPR were urging mass migration to the region, but their efforts had brought few results. Although the land north of Regina to Saskatoon had been surveyed in 1882, nothing much had happened after that. By 1890 there was some settlement for about 30 miles north of Regina, and next to nothing from there north to Saskatoon and beyond to Prince Albert. This was a large and empty landscape crossed by a single railway line. It had been built in 1900 by the Qu'Appelle, Long Lake and Saskatchewan Railway, whose land grants became the foundation of Davidson and McRae's massive prairie-land empire.

The key to their success was to acquire the surplus land rights that had been granted to the railway by the federal government. Mistakenly, the railway company had decided that much of the land that flanked the rail line from Lumsden to Dundurn, between Regina and Saskatoon, was infertile and of little use to anyone. The railway had tried—unsuccessfully—to sell it back to the federal government for $1.25 an acre, but McRae and Davidson knew from discussions with ranchers and grain growers in Minnesota that the land had considerable potential. They talked with local farmers and were further encouraged by what they learned. They took an educated gamble that others could be persuaded to their way of thinking, providing the price of the land was right. With the strength of their convictions they sunk all the money they could raise into a new company. It was incorporated as the Saskatchewan Valley Land Company, headquartered in Winnipeg, with Andrew Davidson as president and McRae as secretary.

McRae sunk every penny he had into the scheme that in a very short time produced great wealth and a mixture of fame, notoriety, envy, and criticism as he made an unbelievable fortune in prairie real estate. The money rolled in so fast and there was so much of it that for the rest of his life, particularly during his political career, McRae was haunted by accusations that there had to be something crooked in the way the sales were handled. Nothing underhanded ever came to light, and in a manner that was characteristic of him, McRae always met the suggestions of wrongdoing head on.

He began work on the Canadian project shortly after his marriage, travelling a great deal back and forth across the country until after Blaunche gave birth to their second daughter in 1904. During those years he and Blaunche maintained a home in Minneapolis where there were men with money to invest, and where Blaunche still had friends and the support of her family during her pregnancies.

During this period, 1901 to 1903, Alexander Davidson remained in Minneapolis in order to supervise the earlier family investments; although, he was also involved in enlisting the support of a syndicate of investors willing to put money into Canadian land. In Winnipeg Andrew and Alexander McRae embarked on a land buying spree, taking advantage of the opportunity to buy land from the Qu'Appelle Railway. Initially they acquired close to a million acres between Regina and Prince Albert for $1.53 an acre. They bought another 100,000 acres from the Saskatchewan Western Railway. Wanting to amass even more if they could find it, because they had been carefully monitoring the rising price of prairie land, the two men approached the federal government with a request to purchase the huge tract they wanted to bring their already sizeable parcels together into one huge holding. Ottawa was most anxious to attract new settlers to the prairies. The Saskatchewan Valley Land Company offered the government a chance to increase colonization. By agreeing to contractual requirements stipulated by the Liberal government aimed at ensuring further settlement, Davidson and McRae were able to acquire the land they wanted for $1 an acre.

The men from Glencoe fine-tuned their negotiating skills during the acquisition of the prairie lands. They were undaunted by the size of the project or the skills of the lawyers and politicians they dealt with, and together had become a formidable management team. They agreed on a vision of the future, combined their talents, and amassed over five million acres of prairie, an area larger than some small European countries. Now came the crucial test. Would the land sell as well as they hoped? They prepared to launch a massive sales campaign, directed towards prospective American investors and settlers.

The Lonely, Magnificent Prairies

The Davidson-McRae plan came to public attention across North America in the spring of 1902 when a steam train huffed-and-puffed its way into Winnipeg, its whistle blowing as it crossed from Minnesota into Manitoba. It carried many of the moneyed men the Davidsons and McRae had attracted as investors in their syndicate. Their arrival in Winnipeg and subsequent trip to Regina, Saskatoon, and Prince Albert marked the beginning of a new chapter in Canadian history: the settlement of the soon-to-be province of Saskatchewan, and the eastern part of the province of Alberta. The partners' objective was to reassure investors the scheme was viable and then to attract those who would purchase land, build homesteads, and grow crops.

Their major sales promotion took the form of two extravagant expeditions designed to reveal the potential of the Canadian prairie to farmers, investors, and politicians from across the continent and to inform the general public of North America there was land for sale, the likes of which they had never seen before. It was May 28 when the first train chugged out of Minneapolis, carrying Alexander McRae and the Saskatchewan Valley Land Company investors.

The Davidsons were waiting in Winnipeg with another group of investors, and it was during the trip west that for the first time they revealed the names of the people who had invested in their scheme and formed the executive board of their new Winnipeg-based firm. Aboard that first train were two key supporters: A.G.Douglas of Cedar Rapids, Iowa, vice-president of Saskatchewan Valley Land and a man widely known in the United States as president of The Quaker Oats Company; and G. F. Piper of Minneapolis, the newly named treasurer of the Winnipeg company and a man credited with raising Midland Linseed Oil Company production to one-fifth or one-quarter of all the linseed oil produced in the United States. Included in the impressive list of directors was McRae's father-in-law (described in one Saskatchewan news sheet as G. F. Howe, Minneapolis millionaire); F.E. Kenaston, president of Minneapolis Threshing Machine Co. and John Abell Engineering Works and also the man formerly involved in the purchase of the Little Falls Granite Company; and Thomas C. Wells of Chicago, president of Continental Packing and vice-president of Quaker Oats. In partnership with T. Hord, Wells owned a 250,000-acre ranch in Nebraska that in the preceding year fed one million bushels of corn to its animals. The list of those associated with the project read like a "who's who" in mid-western banking and agriculture circles and included a couple with Canadian affiliations such as J.W. de Courchy O'Grady, manager of the Bank of Montreal in Chicago.

The Leader was a small weekly broadsheet that to some extent connected the people of tiny Regina with the outside world. Although still much concerned with the health of King Edward in England whose coronation was postponed because of an appendicitis operation, The Leader ran a big story in the spring of 1902 on the formation of the Saskatchewan Valley Land Company, which it described as "the biggest land deal since the CPR." There had been other such proposals and they had come to nothing, said The Leader. It described McRae as a well-known Duluth capitalist involved with others from Minneapolis and from eastern Canada. While enthusiastic about the project, The Leader repeated there had been other people with fancy ideas that had come to naught and reminded readers that a few had made money and moved on quickly; however, the paper added, this new proposal seemed to have some weight behind it.

One week later The Leader told its readers of the first train's arrival. Most aboard this train were key investors in the development company, the reporter noted, and they rolled into town in a unit headed by a private dining car named "Luciana." They came to Canada over the Minneapolis, St. Paul, and Sault Ste. Marie Railway line into Winnipeg before proceeding further west. After meeting up with a Canadian contingent—some from Toronto and Montreal—the train headed for Regina, and an evening's entertainment before attempting the trip north to Prince Albert.

The next day proved to contain a fair share of excitement for the travellers. *The Leader's* reporter said it was exceptionally warm; ten miles from Lindsay the unbearable heat "extended" the rails and the engine left the tracks. It was reported as only a minor mishap, nobody was hurt, but it was ten hours before the rails were repaired and the trip was resumed. The porters and cook on the "Luciana" said it was hotter on the prairie grassland than it had been in South Carolina, a state they had left just a few days earlier. Those aboard the train were soon entranced by the "beautiful rolling tracts of prairie land which looked like a new mown lawn." The land in question extended for 50 miles on one side of the track and fifteen to twenty on the other, "all of it owned by Saskatchewan Valley Land Company."

During the ten-hour wait for the rails to be repaired the men on the train had begun to discuss the future of this fantastic land they had never seen before. They envisioned granaries, mills, and new cities springing up in the midst of fields ripe with wheat and flax. "While sitting around the car one evening no less than 80,000 acres were sold to individual members of the company," stated *The Leader*. With development would come villages and towns. It was decided that one should be named Davidson in honour of the president of the Saskatchewan Valley Land Company. Because one director had purchased so much land, another new town also came into existence: it would be Kenaston. During the two-and-a-half day trip between Regina and Prince Albert, 200,000 acres were sold. Some of the investors bought for themselves and some bought for friends. McRae's father-in-law, G. F. Howe, saw flax as a major crop and soon was discussing plans for building a milling plant in Winnipeg. These men confidently predicted many mid-western American farmers would sell their developed land at a good price and move into Canada to buy new property at bargain prices.

The travellers on the luxury train weren't bothered when the telegraph line went down and they were out of touch with the world. They were on an exciting expedition and the lack of news from the outside gave them more time to ponder and develop their own ideas, weighing their options for the future. The scope of the plans "almost took the breath away of local men," said *The Leader,* explaining that whole new towns were being planned and single farms were described with as much as 23,000 acres under cultivation. One of the entrepreneurs boasted that within five years the land would be worth more than even the best farmland in Ontario. Kenaston said his firm would build a warehouse and machine shop in Winnipeg to serve western Canada and the booming development that now was guaranteed.

The Americans were so enthusiastic about the project, and so impressed with the possibilities for the future, that at the end of an amiable evening en route to Winnipeg during the return trip, Kenaston was moved to propose a toast to the health of the ailing King Edward in an expression of friendship to his Canadian neighbours.

Less than a month later on June 25, a second, larger expedition left Minneapolis destined for Winnipeg, Regina, and points north. On the luxury train were more well-known titans of industry as well as powerful politicians from Minneapolis and points east— 170 in all, along with 30 reporters from across both countries who were wined and dined for nearly a week as the train puffed its way through the unbroken prairie. McRae escorted the group from the mid-west while Andrew and Alexander Davidson— accompanied by Canadian bankers, CPR officials, and politicians —again joined the train at Winnipeg. The two groups continued on to Regina where they arrived on June 27.

The high stakes being risked made the high costs incurred on the two ambitious expeditions an essential part of generating the continent-wide excitement and publicity needed to push the ambitious project forward. The Davidsons and McRae spared no expense. Train rental alone for the two expeditions, which

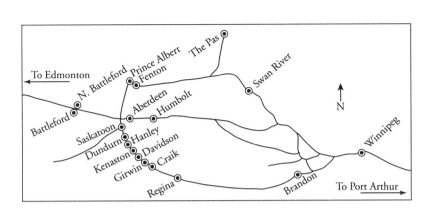

Davidson and McRae became land agents for all the lands acquired by the Canadian Northern Railway, stretching from Manitoba to British Columbia, including not only farmland but also the townsites and city lots that were developed all along the railway's route. The two men often invested in infrastructure for some of the communities, building banks and office buildings in some of the larger centres.

included eight Pullman cars in addition to a dining and baggage car, was $16,000. One source suggested there were 1,500 cigars purchased for the second trip. That meant more puffing than was performed by the train as it chugged its way north. Smoke-filled back rooms were the regular haunts of the entrepreneurs and politicians aboard, but they were soon overwhelmed by the vastness of what they saw: the lands of Saskatchewan. While they gazed in awe the wealthy investors had an opportunity to consume some 3,000 pounds of meat, 500 heads of lettuce, 500 cucumbers, 600 loaves of bread, and more. They drank 25 cases of Apollinaris water, according to newspaper reports, although discreetly there was no listing of the liquor and fine wines that went with the smooth selling pitch of McRae and the Davidsons. To look after their comforts—the cigars, food, and refreshments—the second expedition had four cooks and five waiters in the dining car.

The second expedition into the hinterland was even more flamboyant than the first. McRae and Davidson used all their influence to enhance a star-studded passenger list. This was the trip designed to publicize the scheme throughout North America. They were out to make news and this they did. Aboard the luxury train was Governor S.R. Van Slant of Minnesota, as well as the governor of Iowa, a Supreme Court judge, and bankers from New York, Chicago, and Minnesota. Prominent Canadians aboard were Manitoba Lieutenant-Governor Daniel Hunter, Winnipeg newspaper publisher R.L. Richardson, plus a squad of American and Canadian reporters who were encouraged to tell the almost unbelievable story back home.

McRae and Davidson got the good press they had hoped for. The *Winnipeg Daily Tribune* said that under their smooth handling "everything went as merrily as the proverbial marriage bells ... the Americans learned there is an empire of land in the Canadian North West." The *Tribune* said they were a "genial lot" who enjoyed the good life as they watched through the windows as mile after mile of untouched land rolled by. They were impressed by the lushness of the prairie grass and the obvious fertility of the soil, many noting that it only needed the touch of the plow to make this a home for millions of people. The paper interviewed many of the visitors who had nothing but good things to say about the panorama before them and its possibilities.

Arthur Ford, who was a writer for the *Winnipeg Telegram* and later publisher of the *London Free Press*, revealed how impressed the investors were in his book *As the World Wags On*. He related a colourful tale of the journey and explained what happened when the visitors started to lay purchase orders with McRae. He was "sitting at a table in the dining car, accepting checks as fast as he could write receipts. He had two large waste paper baskets beside him which he used as receptacles for slips of coloured paper, each one representing a different amount of money. Before Saskatoon was reached both baskets were full." There is no doubt a lot of business was done as the train clanked over the tracks, but filling two baskets stretches the imagination. One Chicago banker bought 25,000 acres, the Chicago branch of the Bank of Montreal bought 6,000, and according to the *Tribune*, a minor example of a sale was the initial purchase of

1,000 acres by the Illinois Central Railway. At Prince Albert, three enterprising women boarded the train and extracted $150 from the visitors as donations for the local hospital.

In addition to the sightseeing rail journeys, Davidson and McRae embarked on a massive advertising campaign. Cheap land was the pitch. They bought a two-page supplement in the *Minneapolis Journal* and had copies of it distributed at the Minnesota State Fair. They ran advertisements in nearly 300 other newspapers across the United States and set up a network of 3,000 selling agencies in farming communities across Iowa, Minnesota, and North and South Dakota—the wheat and flax growing lands of the United States. Company representatives also approached potential settlers from Ontario, Quebec, and other parts of Atlantic Canada. The agreement Davidson and McRae had signed with the Canadian government to purchase land at $1 an acre included assurances that every effort would be made to attract new settlers to the North West Territories, and before long, the settlers were rolling in.

The partners became fascinated with their own success as the first actual future settlers began to visit their sales agencies. They were aided by a new, separate drive by the province of Manitoba to draw Americans to that region. The provincial government was concerned that there would be an exodus from Winnipeg and a halt to new settlement and so they advertised that land was available in Manitoba at prices that were a fraction of what similar farms in the United States would cost. Some who visited the Winnipeg area soon learned of the even cheaper prices for land further west. It is probable that the parallel campaigns brought additional settlers to both regions.

All this activity even piqued the interest of *The Globe* in far off Toronto, undoubtedly because some Ontario speculators had already put in offers for land without being too sure what they were buying. *The Globe's* reporter said settlers had brought life into a land that only four years earlier was "as untenanted as Central Asia." The reporter said the first settlers had moved into the Estevan region but that some "adventurous spirits" had moved on farther. He later wrote of his observations from a slight

elevation near the main community. He said with the naked eye
he saw some 110 farmhouses in an area where the land was first
broken in 1899. The first crop year of 1900 had been a disaster
because of drought—always a threat in an area of limited
rainfall—but the original pioneers had managed to stay on the
land and it had produced a bumper crop in 1901. The new settlers
were not to learn fully of the devastating results of long-term
drought until some 30 years later. To many readers of *The Globe*
in Ontario, this was their first promising look at land to the west
where the buffalo once roamed and which many had heretofore
considered inhospitable and uninhabitable.

A book, *Canadian Men and Women of the Time,* written
by Henry James Morgan in 1912, dubbed Davidson as the man
who made the Saskatchewan Valley and described the scheme
developed by the men from Glencoe as one of the greatest
migration movements of modern times. Davidson, never a
shrinking violet, was proud of the assertion that he was the
father of the American invasion of the prairies. He, much more
than McRae, kept a foot in both the Canadian and American
business worlds, always maintaining a home in Duluth. The
book states, "He was an imperialist believing that Canada's great
future and best interests lay along the lines of a nation within
the Empire." He liked his honorary title of colonel, earned for
bringing modern banking practices and safe depositories to
Minnesota, and if anyone assumed he had won it in battle, he
didn't rush to correct them.

The growth in population on the prairies following the
Davidson-McRae campaign was remarkable. Americans poured
in from the south. Davidson received much of the acclaim for
bringing settlers to the flat lands, so much was made of the small
town named after him during the initial railway journey to Prince
Albert. McRae could possibly have chosen a site for a town called
McRae but did not do so, in keeping with his tendency to stay
behind the footlights rather than in their glare.

Today Davidson has a population of 1,117 and is described
as a friendly community with all the amenities of city living,
equipped with a hospital and a regional college sub office. The

town's history as posted on the internet includes the comment, "It is named after Colonel Andrew Duncan Davidson, who was commissioner of the Canadian Northern Railroad for eleven years. As a member of a firm involved in the sale of lands, it is estimated he sold over 15,000,000 acres of land. He is popularly known as 'the man who made the Saskatchewan Valley.'" No mention is made of McRae or any of the others involved with the Saskatchewan Valley Land Company.

By 1903, the small settlements of Davidson and Craik had sprung up between Regina and Saskatoon along with several others, some with populations of more than 200. A year later the village of Davidson boasted two large hotels, two general stores, two hardware stores, a sash and door factory, a blacksmith shop, stables, and even a newspaper called the *Davidson Leader*. It was incorporated as a village in February or March in 1904, and officially became a town in 1906. Davidson and McRae bankrolled some of the building and new businesses as an added inducement for settlement. The men had a magic touch that worked so well that the federal government had to set up an immigration office to handle the large numbers of settlers arriving in the region.

The first settlements, villages, and towns on Saskatchewan lands were isolated and far from major centres, but they were neither lonely nor isolated for long. Instead, they were fast growing ever-changing centres, filled with confident people who were sure of their own futures and the new colonization that was only just beginning. Regina was the biggest centre, destined to become the capital of a new province, with a population of slightly more than 25,000 people by 1902. The city council approved spending estimates for the year of $23,590.76, including $8,000 for schools, which was their largest expenditure. They also earmarked $1,000 for a quarantine hospital and $300 for parks. *The Leader* reported the community was desperately short of building materials, something that McRae—always with an eye out for new opportunities—had already observed. The paper also noted that flooding in Alberta had disrupted communications and delayed a large shipment of lumber from B.C.

There were complaints that if not for the horse racing and sporting events, the Regina Exhibition on August 7 would have been a bust, because there had been a poor display of vegetables and only two city businesses had bothered to enter displays. There was a $125 prize in the main racing event, and awards of $20 and $10 in the baseball contest. In what was labelled as the best game ever seen on the prairies, the city team beat the men of the North West Mounted Police by a score of two to nothing. The city's pitcher, Orr, threw a no hitter, while opposing chucker Walker struck out eighteen and gave up four hits, but the blows were enough for the narrow and very exciting victory. There was a shortage of skilled labour in some sectors. One advertisement offered $1,400 in annual salary and commission for the manager of a 6,000-acre farm along with an eight-room house. The Glasgow House had a sale with parasols going for 70 cents, men's suits selling for half-price at $2.50, coffee for 25 cents a pound, and tea for 50 cents a pound; a rival merchant was offering three pounds of tea for $1.00 while women's button boots were $1.50.

The influx of settlers was hailed by the Regina land office where a spokesman applauded the soaring numbers of applications for homesteads. Apparently 2,309 had been requested between April and September of 1902 compared with 647 for the same period the year before. Author Arthur Ford, however, wrote in his book that not everybody was ecstatic about the newcomers. While his paper reported the optimistic developments, *Winnipeg Tribune* publisher and Member of Parliament R.L. Richardson didn't seem to share the enthusiasm of the Americans and other writers, portraying himself as the quintessential Canadian doubter. Winnipeg was calling itself the gateway to the west and maybe Richardson was not happy with a diversion of resources to these upstarts. *The Tribune* reported that some Manitoba critics claimed it was a "bunco" operation that was selling useless land to gullible Americans, although it was very shortly forced to change its tune.

A major problem in all Canadian development and not just the emerging west was a lack of home-grown capital and the great need to seek it in the United States, England, and other parts of Europe. Ford quotes Richardson, who was on the second train, as saying, "Those fool Yankees can have it all for me; it isn't worth 10-cents an acre." He was sadly wrong. The Americans took a lot of it, bringing a cool nine million dollars to Davidson, McRae, and the other investors in the Saskatchewan Valley Land Company—a great fortune for the times, close to $200 million in today's dollars.

The millions that McRae received as his share of this amazing undertaking had a down side that was to shadow him for the rest of his life. To many envious observers the promoters had made too much too fast. There had been others in Canadian history that made great killings in a short time, notably the top management of the Canadian Pacific Railway and those who made fortunes in the Klondike gold rush of 1898. The railway men despite the scandal, kickbacks, bribery, and political skullduggery had produced a line that tied the country together, and the miners had hauled out gold for all to see. In the eyes of some, McRae and Davidson had been merely opportunists who garnered wealth by manipulating the sale of land that they had acquired too easily. They seemed too smooth, too glib, and too clever for the average Canadian; undoubtedly envy and jealousy coloured the thinking of the average salesman, teacher, secretary, farmer, logger, miner, or factory worker.

The initial response from opposition Conservative politicians in Ottawa was cautious. Some voiced the view that Canada could blacken its name by conning gullible Americans into buying land that was useless and would never grow crops. They described it as a water-starved desert in the summer and an ice-cold, wind-swept Siberian-like expanse of nothing in winter. Manitoban politicians were particularly critical, perhaps sharing Richardson's views that there should be no competition for the scarce amount of capital available for investment.

Clifford Sifton was the Liberal government's Minister of the Interior, charged with attracting immigrants to help fill the great emptiness of the central plains. In the House of Commons on July 19, 1904, he came under a barrage of attack from the opposition. One Conservative member held to the old line that he wouldn't have accepted any of the land even if it were offered for no more than land tax owing on it. Others were more aware of the movement of people and the economic gains being made in the new west. The attack gradually changed direction so that the Conservatives now attacked the government for having given away the land too cheaply, giving a stunning advantage to the Saskatchewan Valley Land Company. There were whispers in parliamentary halls in Ottawa of pay-offs and financial fiddling. The contention was that even if there was no direct evidence, there must be something crooked behind it all. When land bought for as little as $1 an acre was sold for as much as $10 an acre and more, reaping a huge profit for the company and its promoters, something was wrong.

Sifton, with the facts and figures of growth at hand, hit back, saying that much money had been brought to the federal treasury by the actions of the Davidson-McRae team, which had produced results "of immense benefit to the North West." The minister told the House that even if the land had been given to them for nothing it still added up to benefits to Canada "ten times over." He further stated that the coming of their company was "the beginning of the great success of our migration work in the West." Sifton maintained that the company had been exceptionally effective as a colonization agent. "It has placed lots of valuable settlers not only on this tract but on the remainder of its tracts. I can recall no feature of our colonization in the North West which has been attended with greater success than the efforts of this company." There was now "a large and thriving settlement in the area north of Regina," Sifton said, adding, "I think the transaction is in every way advantageous to the country and one which will promote good settlement."

In John Dafoe's book, *Clifford Sifton in Relation to His Times,* the minister was quoted as stating that he saw one farm producing 120,000 bushels of wheat and two that easily grew 40,000. The minister added: "In going through this tract a year ago I saw the land which in the spring of 1902 was absolute desert without anybody and without the means of subsistence for man or beast. I saw on the tract last year villages, elevators, shops, hotels and the largest wheat field I ever saw in my life." Sifton said the project had turned out to be a "pretty fair transaction" for the federal Interior Department. He acknowledged that the company had wanted to make some money "and that is a proper ambition on the part of anybody; I may say it is the ambition that most people have when they go west."

While some critics continued to probe the deal, their efforts produced no evidence of kickbacks or shady financial deals between the promoters, the federal government, or the railway companies that sold the rights and the land. There was, unquestionably, more who hailed the program than there were those who panned it. In *The Story of Saskatchewan and its People,* John Hawkes called it "the most spectacular colonization project in the history of western Canada." A cornerstone had been laid in the central plains, one that was to change the face of the great region as settlements became villages and then towns and cities.

The statistics tell the story of success, and phenomenal growth. In 1901 the population of the whole of the North West Territories was 158,940 and in only five years it had grown to 443,175. The Davidson-McRae colonization project had played a large part in this population increase, giving the year-old provinces of Saskatchewan and Alberta a solid base on which to grow.

By early 1903 sales of the original lands acquired by the Saskatchewan Valley Land Company had dwindled. However, the genius of Andrew Davidson and Alexander McRae had caught the eyes of William McKenzie and Donald Mann, two pioneer railway builders in western Canada. They had launched their Canadian Northern Railway in 1895 after signing contracts with the government of Manitoba. Eventually, with 25 million acres in land rights, their line snaked across Canada and rivalled the Canadian Pacific Railway. The first cross-country rail line went west from Winnipeg, through Calgary to Vancouver, while the Canadian Northern swung northwest from the Manitoba capital into Saskatoon and Edmonton en route to the coast. The northern line travelled the prairies as a private carrier until 1918 when it was sold to the Dominion government and became the federally-owned Canadian National Railway.

McKenzie and Mann approached the principals of the Saskatchewan Valley Land Company late in 1902, and after extensive negotiations a contract was drawn up, creating a new company, The Saskatchewan and Manitoba Land Company, which became exclusive land agents for Canadian Northern. This was a much larger proposition than their original scheme. Signed in Toronto in May 1903, the contract provided an initial 2.1 million acres in land rights. When the contract expired in 1905, Davidson-McRae Land Agents continued to act as agents for the railway, and in the ensuing fifteen years the sales and development of land expanded significantly. The company, acting as selling and development agent for the railway builders, was responsible for selling and encouraging settlement of the land as well as the development of whole communities as the need for them arose. This enterprise encompassed an area many millions of acres more than had their original project. It was a continuing source of revenue for the investors in Davidson-McRae, although neither Andrew Davidson nor Alexander McRae was actually involved in the day-to-day operation of the company after 1906 or 1907. They developed the idea, promoted it, sold it successfully, and then moved on to new more exciting endeavours, leaving other members of the family in charge of the daily operations of Davidson–McRae Ltd.

In his book *The Canadian Northern Railway—Pioneer Road of the Northern Prairie 1895-1918*, T.D. Regehr states that the original agreement called for the railway to receive a guaranteed $3 an acre and 30 percent of profits above this amount. There was an additional proviso that the land would not be sold for less than $5 an acre. In the first two years of operation the new venture, headquartered at bustling Portage and Main in Winnipeg, and with a United States head office in St. Paul, sold some 700,000 acres all well above the $5 floor price. The 3,000 sales offices across the United States were retained, offering land in Manitoba, Saskatchewan, and into Alberta to settlers as well as lots for business development in townsites along the railway route. New sales offices were also opened in eastern Canada and even in Europe.

With the expansion of their enterprise, the Winnipeg-based company was very much in need of new staff to cope with its increased responsibilities. McRae brought his younger brother Randolph to work in Winnipeg. Alexander Davidson, who had managed the sales offices in the United States out of St. Paul, moved in 1906 with his wife and son Rolland to Winnipeg in order to manage the Canadian enterprise and free Andrew Davidson and McRae for other projects. Alexander Davidson managed land sales and industrial development across Saskatchewan, Alberta, and into B.C. until the company's demise; but Randolph, perhaps wanting to achieve something on his own, travelled to South America in search of his own future. He unfortunately met an untimely death under mysterious circumstances that were never satisfactorily explained.

A sales brochure printed in 1910 about Davidson–McRae Land Agents unashamedly quotes an unnamed and boastful American as stating, "Canada is the only country that has proved good enough for the Americans to migrate to." The language is condescending, but the American dollar was good. The agents said more than 90,000 Americans migrated to Canada in 1909, and the number was expected to total 170,000 by the end of 1910. Davidson–McRae predicted in its promotional material that land going for $20 an acre would be valued at $100 in ten years. The brochure extolled the promise, "The prairies of the Canadian West are a delight to all those who see them, stretching away in the distance for miles without number, seemingly having no bounds. They become more interesting, however, as you get better acquainted with them and know their worth. The great plains, where once the ranchman held sway, are rapidly becoming converted into a rich agricultural country, the home of prosperous and wealthy farmers. The enormous amount of construction done in the past by the Canadian Northern Railroad has opened up huge tracts of the finest portions of these prairies, furnishing facilities to hundreds of thousands of immigrants and new settlers for acquiring at least the nucleus of independence."

Some of those who settled on the prairies and over the years faced months of freezing, winter isolation, summer drought, dust storms, and infestations of insects that consumed their hard-worked crops, as well as the devastating Depression of the 1930s, might have wondered at times if this independence was worth the price. Of all the Americans, Ukrainians, and others from Europe brought in to populate the plains, however, most stayed despite the bad years, forging a future for their descendants who today make the Great Plains flourish in ways that the pioneers could not have dreamed.

Agents Davidson and McRae continued to facilitate the process, but one project envisioned by Mackenzie and Mann was to haunt McRae in future years and make him a target of political attack. In 1910 the Canadian Northern promoters announced they had acquired two-and-a-half miles of Fraser River waterfront east of New Westminster where they planned to build huge maintenance workshops for their railway equipment serving the Pacific coast. Some of the land was also available for public sale, so Davidson–McRae Land Agents put it on the market. Many people in the Vancouver area, believing it was a sound investment, scrambled to buy. Lots close to this proposed, large industrial development seemed destined to be money-makers in years to come. Instead, many lost money when Mackenzie and Mann—the area named after the latter as Port Mann—had a change in plans, and the proposed workshops were cancelled. The machine shops were never built and land values plummeted. Years later when McRae entered politics he was accused of having profited grandly in a land scheme that cost others money. He always insisted he was merely an inactive partner by the time this proposal came forward and added that no one could have predicted the workshop project would not go ahead.

McRae remained active in the company only until 1906 when Alexander Davidson moved to Winnipeg in order to take over management of land sales and development. Within a year, both McRae and Andrew Davidson had moved on to the west coast in search of new adventures and broader horizons.

Alexander Davidson continued to manage Davidson and McRae's interests until 1918 when the Canadian Northern Railway became part of the Canadian National Railway system. Both he and his wife Laura died in Winnipeg, she in 1917 and he in 1922. Both bodies were shipped back to Little Falls, Minnesota for burial where Laura's family, the Tanners, had been one of the pioneers in the original development of that community.

Alexander Davidson was well remembered in Little Falls as a banker and a large farming landowner. In his obituary the *Little Falls Daily* said he had a large circle of friends, a genial disposition together with an unusual memory for names and faces, and was known by a large proportion of the earlier residents of Morrison County. He was praised for "his strong personality, his optimism and perhaps above all, his abounding cheerfulness … forever cherished in memory."

In less than five years the Davidsons and McRae had made an unfathomable success of the Saskatchewan Valley Land Company and its successor projects, but they were always working on new ideas, seeking new places to reinvest their now sizable fortunes. They both turned their eyes west, seeing in British Columbia the greatest possibilities for the future.

When McRae made a rail trip to the coast in 1905 his first view of bustling, brash Vancouver filled him with excitement. He loved his first sight and smell of the broad Pacific Ocean and the view of the mountains that could be seen from nearly everywhere in the city. It was also filled with people with close ties to Great Britain, particularly to Scotland. It was a city where he immediately felt he belonged. And there were huge trees on the coast, capable of supplying lumber that was needed in substantial amounts for prairie home building. Here was a city with the kind of attitude he liked and now he had the kind of money to influence its success as well as his own. His mind immediately filled with ideas for the future, and he decided to move there as soon as possible.

Blaunche and their two daughters had moved to Winnipeg in 1904 when it became more apparent that Alexander would spend more and more of his time in Canada. Blaunche immediately established a reputation for herself as an accomplished equestrian. She won a series of competitions, and she and Alexander hosted a number of lavish parties for prominent young people in the Manitoba capital. Local newspapers frequently covered her appearances at receptions and fetes, describing her stylish clothes in glowing terms. She was a young, beautiful woman from the United States with a very wealthy husband and she made an impression wherever she appeared. It was not long, however, before she was once again pregnant, expecting a third child early in 1906. McRae was ready to move on to Vancouver but realized he should wait until after the child was born. He set his sights on late 1906 or 1907. In the meantime he scouted out new business prospects in British Columbia, and took a look at the residential real estate market, deciding the West End was the neighbourhood Blaunche would probably prefer. It was home to most of the city's wealthy families, many of them—like McRae—with newly made fortunes.

While Vancouver had the atmosphere and vitality McRae sought, and the resources he needed to expand his wealth, it also had a host of problems of which he was not fully aware when he and his family took up residence on Nicola Street in the West End in 1907. A key factor affecting life in Vancouver, which was not evident elsewhere in Canada to the same extent, was increasing racial tension between the growing "Oriental"— the term used at this time to refer to Chinese, Japanese, and natives of India—community and the rest of the Lower Mainland population. An economic downturn pitted new immigrants from Great Britain against young Orientals vying in the job market for employment as domestics, in restaurants, on fish boats, in lumber camps, or in mining operations. The Chinese majority bore the brunt of the anti-Asian prejudice.

Chinese Riots

The Chinese first arrived from the Orient in the mid-1800s, seeking to cash in on the gold rushes on the Fraser River and in the B.C. Interior. They readily found a place among the other immigrants from Great Britain and Europe who settled the province in the early years. A great fear of the "yellow peril" did not become evident until Prime Minister Sir John A. Macdonald decided to permit thousands to come from China to lay rail lines in the mountains and canyons of B.C., providing the Canadian Pacific Railway with the men it needed to push the line through to the coast. The prime minister said that without them there would be massive delays in completing the line that was a cornerstone of the new confederation.

The Chinese came and many lost their lives working along the dangerous canyons and tunnelling through the coastal mountain range; some were victims of the highly volatile dynamite that was used. After the line was built and the first train arrived in Vancouver in 1887, many of the Chinese stayed on, most moving to Vancouver where a growing Chinatown became established. The British-born labourers and tradesmen, who formed a large part of the city's population, vehemently complained that the Chinese would work for next to nothing and frequently took jobs away from them. Whenever employment was scarce there was open hostility between the two groups. The Chinese were often employed as domestic servants, fruit and vegetable peddlers, laundrymen, fishermen, miners, and labourers; these were the employment sectors where the union men and farm boys from the old country sought work upon arriving in the city.

Although there was an established niche in Vancouver society for the Chinese, racial prejudice against this large and visible minority resurfaced every time there was a downturn in the local economy. In 1890 Vancouver city council offered a hefty subsidy to the B.T. Rogers Sugar Company to build a refinery in the city. In his book, *The Refiners*, author John Schreiner states a proviso was that the "company shall not at any time employ Chinese labour in and about the said works." Rogers readily agreed. This was four years after the founding of Vancouver and the great fire of 1886 that destroyed much of the downtown community.

The Chinese seldom ventured into Stanley Park or tried to socialize in the city, living apart in a tightly-knit community with their own people and a different culture. Most did not speak English well, if at all, and found it difficult to communicate effectively with the white population. The fear of the Chinese felt by some in the white community was based on a great deal of misinformation about practices taking place in Chinatown relating to opium dens, gambling, and prostitution, much of it exaggerated by daily newspapers.

By the time Alexander McRae and Andrew Davidson set their sights and their futures on B.C., there was no shortage of recruits for the newly founded Asiatic Exclusion League, which wanted all those born of Asian descent banned from Canada, even those who had been born in the country. Membership in the League came from all levels of society, including politicians, clergymen, bankers, doctors, lawyers, businessmen, teachers, tradesmen, loggers, and blue-collar workers. The League had a common aim: white supremacy. This was a time when no Asian could become a Canadian citizen. Under the laws of the land they were not and could not be classed as Canadians. With no rights, they were an easy scapegoat to be blamed for all the woes of the community.

The McRae family's arrival in Vancouver in 1907 coincided with the worst racial riots the city had ever known. The population of about 50,000 had become increasingly upset with the Asians and their incursions into what was termed British society. Trouble was triggered by a meeting called by the Asiatic Exclusion League on September 9, which began with a flag-waving parade through the streets of the downtown area. The crowd was estimated at about 8,000 when it reached city hall. A couple of church ministers delivered fiery speeches and the mob grew angrier by the minute, demanding drastic action by the federal government to change immigration laws because the "yellow peril" had invaded the city. Newly arrived workers worried about losing their jobs while business owners had conflicting feelings. They were concerned about losing a source of good cheap labour, but were careful not to voice their concerns about this too loudly. A few also had fears of emerging competition from growing Chinese enterprises.

One view expressed by the white men was not disputed: white women were in increasing danger of sexual assault from "Orientals" who lusted after their bodies. Police records did not verify this supposition.

Following the inflammatory rhetoric delivered by the churchmen, an irate shouting phalanx broke away from the gathering and rampaged along Pender Street, smashing store windows in the heart of Chinatown, looting, and beating up any Chinese who were caught on the streets. The mob then turned its wrath on the smaller Japanese community that lived nearby. The Japanese, however, were prepared. The barricades were up, and they weren't about to give in easily. There was some damage and scuffling before the mob returned to Chinatown where it dispersed when confronted by a wall hastily thrown up by beleaguered police and fire departments.

The next day a visiting Japanese government official demanded protection for his country's nationals living in Vancouver. Still, fear and prejudice raged uncontrolled and many citizens believed a story that an army of thousands of Japanese was in hiding, preparing to sweep down on the city. Civic officials demanded protection for the city's residents. The riot became a national issue with wires to and from Ottawa demanding that order be restored. Ottawa's promise to look into the immigration question was of no great satisfaction to anyone. The population wanted more than just assurances that the flood of Orientals impinging on their way of life would be stopped. Prime Minister Sir Wilfrid Laurier sent a wire to Tokyo, assuring the Japanese government that its nationals would be protected.

Taking a leaf from the Japanese, Chinatown residents turned their area into a fortress to beat off any new attacks. They barricaded their shattered homes and collected bricks and bottles for makeshift weapons. There could have been loss of life in a worsened situation if police had not intercepted more than 100 rifles and ammunition that Chinese in so-far peaceful New Westminster tried to smuggle into Vancouver. The riots produced no deaths, but there were some minor injuries. The police arrested some Chinese and some white rioters for various offences. The eventual sentences handed down were little more than slaps-on-the-wrist.

The Chinese, however, struck their heaviest blow the following day by calling a strike. No one showed up for work either in the city or in nearby lumber camps as word spread of the riots. The wealthy were suddenly without the domestic help of houseboys and cooks who lived in the "Chinaman's room" in their basements;

clothes stayed unwashed in locked laundries; home delivery of produce stopped; many mills fell silent; cookhouse meals deteriorated; restaurants closed; and hotel guests found themselves lugging their own baggage and sleeping in unmade beds. Many of these services were jobs that white men declined to fill. Vancouver suddenly became very aware of the impact of the Asian community on its every day life and economy. Having made their point, and with the racial tension easing, the Chinese went back to work. They eventually received close to $100,000 in damages to repair the ravages to their community, and the Japanese were compensated for a lesser loss.

The city banned a proposed meeting of the Exclusion League, which went ahead nevertheless; but it was a subdued affair that drew only a small audience and confined itself to passing a motion blaming the Board of Trade for having encouraged the Chinese. The Board promptly denied the accusation. Many white residents were genuinely ashamed of the violence that took place.

The riots were over, but the memories remained and in the aftermath Vancouver suffered criticism from the media across Canada and in the United States for its racial intolerance. The federal government investigated the issue, realized the still existent attitude of the majority of B.C.'s population, and eventually took action. There were some who said it was wrong. However, most approved an increase in the immigration head tax to a hefty $500. The Asian Immigration Act, which banned all Asians from entering the country, was also imposed in 1923 and was not repealed until 25 years later.

The Asiatic Exclusion League continued to hold meetings, and new Vancouverite Alexander Duncan McRae became a member, along with many others from all walks of life who felt threatened economically or culturally by the "yellow peril." He employed Asians in many of his business enterprises, but it was his unabashed assertion that he never had a Chinese work in his home. The fact he had brought his family to a city where a racial riot had taken place and where prejudice against Asians, particularly the Chinese, was so strong made him take every precaution possible to protect them from harm.

The McRaes Move to Hycroft

By 1909 Vancouver was in the midst of a ten-year period that has been described as "The Golden Years" or "The Gaudy Years," and ended only with the declaration of war in 1914. It was a period when Edwardian opulence was in vogue. Many men, particularly those with the Canadian Pacific Railway (CPR), became wealthy as land speculation and industrial development provided huge profits for those who had capital to invest in land or to start a profitable business before the days of income taxes. And those who made it spent it in newly established men's clubs or in the posh Leyland or Strand Hotel dining rooms or perhaps with their wives at Allen's Restaurant. Each establishment prided itself on impeccable service, and the wealthy clientele demanded it.

The city's population in 1910 was 93,700; by 1913 it had climbed to 134,000, excluding those who lived in Point Grey or South Vancouver, which were separate municipalities. About 250 miles of streetcar line had been laid, and by 1910 the original Granville Street Bridge had been replaced by a swing span. Both it and the Cambie Bridge fed commuters into the suburbs on streetcars electric equipped with long side seats. Several sidings had been built where trams sat and waited for the car coming in the opposite direction to pass. The wooden bridges across False Creek were built on pilings; the streetcars shared them with early motor vehicles as well as horses and carts, which made a terrible clatter when they hurried down Cambie or Granville hills and rolled onto the trestles. In 1911 the new post office was completed at Granville and Hastings and became one of the busiest federal depots in the country. The same year a lot two blocks away on Hastings Street sold for $4,000. It had been purchased in 1886 for eight dollars.

Many of the city's beautiful homes and gardens were located in the West End, among them the Rogers' place "Gabriola" on Davie Street, and "The Strands" on Harwood, owned by H.G. Bell-Irving. To the south, up Granville Street, the CPR had just begun the development of a new residential neighbourhood to be known as Shaughnessy Heights, touted as "the most wonderful residential section of Vancouver's future," the brainchild of CPR President Thomas Shaughnessy. In 1909 heavy clearing had begun, resulting in a bleak hilltop described by one newspaper as a battlefield full of shell holes and void of trees. A total of 1,200 men had worked to clear the site, which was bounded by Sixteenth Avenue, Oak, Forty-First Avenue, and Arbutus Street. Many of the avenues such as Angus, Hudson, Osler, and Nanton—named after prominent men in the CPR—ran into the circular roadway called The Crescent, which circled Angus Park, the location of the largest properties.

In 1909, the first palatial home—for Richard Marpole of the CPR—was nearing completion. Thomas Shaughnessy was building one of the first 46 houses for himself on Angus Drive. Although he spent most of his time in Montreal, Shaughnessy wanted the development to sell well and knew there would be more incentive to achieve this if he built a large home for himself in the centre of the neighbourhood. It was really only a summer place for his family, but opulent nonetheless.

After two years in the city Alexander Duncan McRae decided his family home would be built in this spacious new neighbour-hood. His first tour of the development was in the company of J.E. McMullen, solicitor for the CPR, who had moved to Vancouver from Montreal in 1906, only a year before McRae arrived. They had met at the Vancouver Club and remained friends for the rest of their lives.

All the lots in Shaughnessy were large, many of them two or three acres in size, but only a few offered a view over the city. McRae asked McMullen to help him search them out. There was some view from the land on the north side of The Crescent where the houses would face Angus Park, and it was one of the most desirable areas, but McRae chose instead land behind this just to the north on the brow of the hill. He bought several lots, a total of five and a half acres, enough to ensure his view would not be obscured and to provide space for the kind of elaborate gardens, greenhouses, stables, and driveways favoured by the very rich in Great Britain and on the eastern United States seaboard. He was determined to build something just as fine for himself: the mansion he would call "Hycroft."

Then, as now, wide, winding avenues and villa-like mansions characterized the neighbourhood. The very smallest lot was nearly a half-acre in size. The streets were not laid out in straight lines but followed the contours of the land. They were all wide, with long sweeping curves, some divided by boulevards. To this day these tree-lined avenues present a beautiful setting for the elegant Victorian-Edwardian residences that remain a part of the district. In 1922 a Shaughnessy Heights Building Renovations Act, passed by the provincial government, removed the neighbourhood from municipal control in order to preserve its character and ensure it remained a park-like setting restricted to one-family dwellings on large lots. Although later modified, much of the original character of the area has been retained.

From 1908 to 1914 some 230 mostly palatial homes were being built in Shaughnessy Heights. For years the area resounded with the buzzing of saws and banging of hammers. McRae's home was one of the largest to be built. The first workmen arrived at his site in 1909, but Hycroft was not completed until 1911. There is some controversy as to who designed Hycroft. It was thought until 1981 to have been the Seattle architectural firm of Sommervell and Putnum, who had designed a nearby home called "Shannon." However, in later years this belief was questioned by an architectural student, Linda Lines, who made the argument that the architect was more likely Thomas Hooper who had opened a Vancouver office in 1907 and had previously been responsible for designing many large and magnificent homes in Edmonton and Winnipeg, where McRae had seen some

Begun in 1909, McRae's 30-room mansion, Hycroft, was not completed until 1911 when the family took up residence. It is pictured here nearing completion. Even the stables, fronted by four columns, are adorned with a widow's walk atop the entrance.

of his work. Her argument included a description of the house as Richardson Romanesque, which represented the American style of Victorian architecture found on the eastern seaboard of the United States as well as in Canada. Lines believed McRae was emulating the merchant princes in the United States when he built his palace to include the grandeur of Greek columns, the permanence of concrete smothered in ivy, and the hipped roof covered with green ceramic tile. Hycroft is full of the "symbols of success, permanence and money," she said. A sketch by Thomas Hooper done for McRae bears a remarkable resemblance to the finished product.

McRae spent about $10,000 for the five and a half acre property and built his mansion for about $100,000. It was fronted by ten pillars, elaborate wide outdoor staircases and terraces, and there were another six pillars at the entrance reached via a gateway and circular drive located in what is actually the rear of the house. In the centre of the drive was a statue and fountain surrounded by an elaborate rose garden. There were roses everywhere.

McRae hired landscape architects from the eastern United States to lay out the formal gardens surrounding his home, but implementation of the walkways and gardens was left to local contractors. The gardens featured pergolas, arbors, and statuary as well as exotic imported trees and flowers. The Italian garden became one of the family's favourites: a place of terraces and lawns where all the flowers were blue and yellow in colour and Blaunche McRae, wearing a dress of a matching hue, often created an unforgettable portrait as she entertained her friends.

The house contains 30 rooms on three floors and among them on the lower level are a large ballroom with an adjacent kitchen, a full-sized lounge, bar, and a wine cellar capable of holding 2,000 bottles. On the main level the architect designed an enormous formal two-storey entrance hall running the full width of the mansion and featuring a double staircase, rising to the upper hallway. The main floor also features a large formal drawing room, a conservatory, a billiard room, a library, and two dining rooms, separated by a folding wall so that children could eat with the adults or be fed on their own, depending on the nature of the event. There was also a large kitchen and servants' dining room, several bathrooms, and solariums. The family bedroom suites, guest rooms, and children's quarters filled the second floor, and the servants quarters were at the top of the house under the eaves and the green tiled roof.

By the time the house was completed, the stables for the family horses were nearing completion and a garage for four

cars was being built. The stables were two-storeys tall and built in the same style as the main house, but standing at right angles to it. Blaunche McRae personally oversaw the completion of its stalls and tack room. Both she and Alexander were experienced equestrians and she knew just what she wanted for their animals that had been shipped from Winnipeg where they were purchased. Blaunche often participated in horse shows in Vancouver; Seattle, Washington; and Salem, Oregon while McRae himself competed in equestrian events held in the Horse Show building at Georgia and Gilford. He often rode in shows there with his friend and colleague, B.T. Rogers. This old Vancouver landmark was destroyed by fire in 1960.

A separate building housed an indoor swimming pool, squash courts, and a bowling alley, and there were also outdoor badminton and tennis courts. McRae's three daughters had a playhouse to match the main building, located in the Italian garden near a gazebo where their mother often served tea. Three large greenhouses provided flowers for the house year round, and below the concrete wall at the bottom of the lawns and gardens was an extensive vegetable garden, now the site of an apartment building. The road leading from the crescent to Hycroft was named McRae Avenue, the city of Vancouver's only permanent acknowledgement of this "merchant prince."

The McRaes had moved into 804 Nicola Street in the West End when they first arrived in Vancouver and remained there until their palatial new home in Shaughnessy was completed. While she waited Blaunche McRae made several trips to Europe, particularly to Italy and to Bavaria, where the estate of the former Prince Ludwig II was for sale. Here she purchased some of the magnificent furniture and art treasures that were to fill her home and had them shipped back to Vancouver. She had promised Alexander a home that would equal the chateaus of Europe.

The aerial view shows the scope of the original estate with its vegetable garden in the foreground (now the site of the apartment complex, Hycroft Towers), and with Angus Park, circled by The Crescent, in the background.

55

Some of the final touches before the family took up residence at Hycroft were installation of the huge lanterns atop the big iron gates as well as the roman bath and fountain surrounded by the circular garden and carriageway. There were extensive terraces at the front and sides of the house, and it was not until a year later that the gardens were nearly complete.

Just before the family moved in they visited the site late one evening in order to view Vancouver's celebrations for the coronation of King George V on June 22, 1911. Five giant bonfires were lit in Vancouver to mark the occasion and the most visible one was on the hill at Hycroft in the still unfinished gardens. On that night of celebration the fire lit up the sky, blazing above the city. McRae had taken his whole family to see the spectacle from the best vantage point he knew and also, no doubt, to ensure the fire didn't get out of control. Blaunche was on hand to be sure the noise and flames and the shouts of celebrants didn't spook the horses. For McRae's daughters—Blanche, Lucile, and Margaret (Peggy)—it was exciting to be up so late and to realize they would soon be living in the huge black building etched in the night sky behind the giant bonfire. Late that summer, when the girls were aged eight, six, and five, the family finally moved to Hycroft, high on the hill, overlooking the city.

The house, its auxiliary buildings, and the grounds required a staff of ten, plus a cook and master gardener just to maintain them on a daily basis. The family entertained lavishly on weekends using the main floor reception rooms and dining rooms, or the ballroom downstairs all lit by sparkling crystal chandeliers. Much of the time during the week they lived on the second floor where both Mr. and Mrs. McRae each had their own suites of rooms, each with its own sitting room, bedroom and dressing room—his on the southeastern end of the building and hers on the northwestern end. This idea of separate suites of rooms for a husband and wife was a practice popularized by European royalty and emulated by the very wealthy families of the eastern United States. Although it was originally introduced to permit a certain amount of private philandering, it did not at this time necessarily indicate any estrangement between a husband and wife. It was more an indication of status and wealth.

The children's and guest rooms were between Alexander's and Blaunche's suites. Hycroft was a magical fairyland for the three McRae girls who spent their childhood playing hide and seek in the nooks and crannies of the second floor amongst the antique furniture and velvet draperies.

Stained glass had been made for the atrium at the top of the main staircase. The McRae family crest was emblazoned there above the landing. It consisted of three thistles and the motto, Fortitudine Nec Curo Nec Careo: "With Courage I Shall Have No Want Or Care." It was a motto by which McRae lived. There is no question the family wanted for nothing, but their lives were not without care, sickness, and tragedy.

McRae's magnificent wood panelled billiard room where he entertained his friends and business associates held one of the secrets of the house. There was one oak panel in the wall that could be pushed until it moved as a door and opened directly into the library. When closed, the door was invisible from both the billiard room and the library.

The second floor bathrooms and solariums were added to the house ten years after it was originally built. They are very sumptuous, designed with extraordinary care. In McRae's suite was a jetted shower and steam room. Blaunche's bath held a tub nearly big enough for swimming, decorated in green and white tile. Huge ferns stood in the corners where they were reflected in the full-length mirrors as well as those built in above the dressing table. Her bedroom was papered in pink bows and plumes and next to it was the blue solarium where she played mahjong in the afternoons.

The gardens surrounding the home were laid out and planted around the huge sequoia tree that McRae acquired specifically for the front of the house. The hill had been stripped bare of trees before Hycroft was built, so McRae went looking for trees. He wanted large ones as well as saplings. When he decided on the sequoia, his friends told him it was too big to transplant, but he would not be deterred. When he wanted something he usually got it. He also planted a copper beech tree, which has grown to become the largest in western Canada, and two davidia trees that came from the Orient and continue to flourish.

There were vast lawns in front of the mansion, and flowers bloomed in the beds continuously from early spring until late fall. In spring there were hundreds of tulips and daffodils raising their brilliant heads to the sun, and by June the scent of roses filled the air. The grounds were laid out to include several different styles of formal gardens. The Italian garden, for example, was characterized by brick walkways and rose gardens. Blaunche McRae insisted that all its flowers be either blue or yellow, and the gardeners were careful to implement her colour scheme. The Italian garden was fairly close to the house and was built to complement the roman terraces surrounding the home. It was adorned with Romanesque statues standing on the lawns around which the family often played croquet. Some of the statues were brought from Italy and others were done locally.

For some time an Italian artist, a sculptor named Carlos Marega, worked in the house and gardens. He came from Trieste but had moved to Vancouver about the time Hycroft was being built. When he became a Canadian citizen he changed his name from Carlos to Charles. He carved one of the fireplaces as well as the plaster relief work on some of the ceilings. Most of the other fireplaces were imported from Italy. Marega became very well-known in Vancouver before the First World War and was responsible for much of the ornamentation on the Burrard Bridge as well as the lions at Lions Gate Bridge and some of the statuary in Stanley Park.

The house, more like a Roman villa than anything else in Vancouver at the time, was designed for elaborate entertaining. Before the First World War and during the 1920s and early 1930s, the winter social season in Vancouver began about the first day of October. It was filled with house parties held at all the grand mansions, all of which had names. William Lamont Tait lived not far from Hycroft at "Glen Brae" on Matthews, and H.R. MacMillan resided at "Duart" on Hudson. Lily Lefevre was the first to move away from both the West End and Shaughnessy when some years later she built "Langaravine" on Northwest Marine Drive.

The extensive gardens at Hycroft originally covered some five acres and were adorned with many fountains and statues. There was even a children's playhouse built in the style of the main building with its own green tiled roof. The Italian garden was the site of many afternoon tea parties and receptions. In spring, it was resplendent with tulips and in summer, with roses.

The main drawing room at Hycroft, one of the largest rooms in the mansion, was often the venue for Saturday night parties hosted by Alexander and Blaunche McRae. The windows on the right overlook the terrace and gardens, and the doors at the end of the room lead to the main floor solarium.

Vancouver's high society emulated the Edwardian era in its own particular way. It was a time when women seldom had careers, especially women whose families had money, and so they spent their time arranging teas and dances, and often devoted their talents to organizing charity events. The teas were afternoon affairs where women and young girls wore bright flowered dresses, white gloves, and big picture hats. The weekend parties were always formal affairs, so they dressed to go out for dinner or to a dance. No well-to-do young woman could manage on less than five or six full-length gowns. Newspapers religiously reported the names of everyone who attended the larger events.

The dances and parties at Hycroft were without equal because no one had a ballroom to match the size of the one McRae built. He had heard it said that "the size and opulence of a stately home's ballroom was a measure of the owner's importance" and he had built his own accordingly. He had seen the enormous ballroom when he visited the Vanderbilt home, "Marble House" in Newport, Rhode Island. It was a North

Like her daughter Blaunche, Mama Howe was an ardent horsewoman. A frequent Hycroft guest, she extended her visit to Vancouver during the First World War to be with her daughter and granddaughters while McRae served overseas. Pictured on the right (left to right) are Peggy, Mrs. Howe, Blanche, Mrs. McRae, and Lucile.

American palace and was said to have influenced the building of large homes all over the continent, including Hycroft.

A friend of Mrs. McRae once commented, "You couldn't refuse to dine there even if the invitation came the night before. It was an honour to be invited, almost a royal command." She described the McRaes as the absolute leaders of Vancouver society. "They were fast and really knew how to have fun," she said. They were always trying something new, be it a new game, a new dance, some different type of food, a new place for a vacation, or a new kind of party. Blaunche McRae was famous for the way she filled the house with flowers. The colours were carefully chosen for the occasion or the room where they would be displayed and the smell was often described as intoxicating. The greenhouses behind the stables on the east side of the garden produced magnificent blossoms year long, in part due to the readily accessible supply of manure fertilizer.

In addition to the display of fresh flowers, the walls inside Hycroft were ornately decorated. The ballroom walls as well as those in the major hallways were covered with tapestries, mostly pastoral landscape scenes. Where there were no tapestries, the walls were covered with murals in muted, sometimes sombre shades, which had been painted on canvas and then applied to the walls. Guests at times suggested the murals gave the house a moody, eerie atmosphere, but Blaunche found them subdued and tasteful. The children's view was different. For them the beautiful scenes became imaginative backdrops for their daydreams. A very young Blanche once commented, "You could sit in front of any of them and imagine you were a beautiful maiden going on an exciting adventure in a strange far-off land."

The ballroom was used for gala dinners as well as dancing. Cooks served piping hot meals from the downstairs kitchen while the orchestra sat just beside the curve of the stairs and the music began when the first guests arrived. Beside the ballroom, opposite the stairs, was the lounge where guests retired after dinner while the tables were cleared away in preparation for dancing. The ballroom floor was quite famous. Seaweed had been layered under it as a cushion to make it more resilient, and it was sometimes described as the perfect floor, the very best place to dance the night away. Hycroft parties frequently went into the wee small hours when guests were served consommé from a big silver tureen just before they departed for home. During the 1920s and early 1930s the parties became legendary, especially the grand masked balls held on New Year's Eve.

McRae's nearly twenty-foot-long bar was located at the far end of the lounge. It was quite high and made of polished mahogany with a brass rail just above the floor where a weary dancer could rest his polished patent shoe. The entire room was panelled in glass that shone like diamonds, reflecting crystal glasses and cut glass goblets filled with ruby red wine. From the end of the bar a covered walkway led to McRae's Mews, the recreation complex and swimming pool that had a gallery for spectators who laughed and cheered whenever important matches were taking place. Famous visitors included the Prince of Wales along with other lesser members of the royal family, several governors general, and the B.C. Lieutenant Governor John Nichol, who was a close friend of Alexander McRae.

One of the most frequent visitors was "Mama Howe," McRae's mother-in-law, a lively, outgoing individual with a style all her own. She travelled each year from her home in Minneapolis to spend Christmas and New Year's Eve at Hycroft, and she was often an honoured guest at the masked balls. Her home in Minnesota was a second home to the McRae girls, two of whom had been born there.

Charlie Major's Sequoia Tree

McRae was very proud of his sequoia tree and often told the story of how he had acquired it and the initial odds against its survival. At the time almost everyone in town had heard about McRae's sequoia and quite a number had watched as it wended its way from New Westminster down Kingsway to Sixteenth Avenue and then along Marpole to the new building site on Shaughnessy hill. Charlie Major also delighted in telling the story of how he came to sell it.

"I knew the minute he saw the tree that McRae wanted it. He was building a huge mansion in the new subdivision that the CPR was opening up for those with lots of money. They called it Shaughnessy after one of the company bigwigs. He had only been in Vancouver a couple of years, but everybody knew that Alexander Duncan McRae had a bundle of money he had made on the prairies. His house wasn't going to be like anybody else's and neither were the grounds. They blasted everything off the slope of his property and I knew he wasn't the type who was prepared to wait forever for things to grow again.

"Of course this tree was different; it fitted the bill for McRae who always wanted to be different in his own way. It wasn't a B.C. tree but a sequoia I had brought in from Oregon, you could only get them there or in northern California. It was a young beauty about 20 feet tall and these are trees that grow to 200 feet and more and live for hundreds of years. McRae wanted something that would stand out and become a landmark so everyone would know this was Hycroft. He wanted something that would put its roots down deep, outlive him and maybe whole generations of McRaes. My sequoia was the perfect answer.

"Like me he was a former Ontario farm boy. I was born near Sarnia in 1839, got the west coast gold fever and came out in 1859. It wasn't easy being a pioneer, and it was a long, hard trip to get to the Pacific coast. Along with three others I trekked through the Isthmus of Panama before catching a sailing ship that beat its way north. This part of the world wasn't even a province when I arrived. I worked the Fraser River goldfields without ever hitting a really big stake and turned my hand to many things. At one time I became well-known as a fearless stagecoach driver in the Interior although I wasn't always as brave as I might have seemed. It wasn't easy whipping a team along those mountain tracks with a long drop to the canyon below on one side if you didn't make the bends in the road. But I made money and then I moved south to New

One of the legacies Alexander Duncan McRae left to Hycroft is the giant sequoia tree that still stands on the grounds. Now 100 years old, it soars 100 feet above the garden.

Westminster about 1892. I got into merchandising and real estate, and built what was said to be one of the area's better houses.

"I like gardening so I landscaped the huge property pretty well, grew lots of flowers, planted trees including a few foreign ones that you don't see much in B.C. That's how the sequoia came to be here. McRae heard about my place and my trees and came for a look. He liked it right off the bat and wanted it. I'm no great tree expert but there were people around who knew quite a bit and told him it would never live through another transplant. Still McRae was determined, and he was used to getting what he wanted. He took the advice of Ed Vance, an Englishman who had arrived on the coast quite recently and had been a landscaper for years. He thought it could be done. McRae made me a good offer and I took it, telling him there were no guarantees. If it died after it was moved that was his misfortune. I'm not about to say what he paid for it, but I'm told that by the time that tree was back in the ground at Shaughnessy, McRae hadn't much left out of $400. For that money he could have bought himself a whole forest. But it was the sequoia he wanted.

"McRae had a long, flat rig made for the trip. My crew had to dig down really deep to make sure they got all the roots and Ed Vance had them build a kind of necklace of logs that they put around the roots and then hauled the tree onto the rig. Headed by a policeman on a horse this strange looking sight took off trundling west along the Kingsway logging road to Vancouver. It was pulled by a ten-horse team and a lot of people looked and wondered what it was about and what was going on. It was a good fifteen miles to Shaughnessy and it took the best part of a day. They had an equally big hole dug at Hycroft. The log necklace was removed and the sequoia had made the trip in good shape. McRae watched as they planted it right where he wanted it at his new place. He made sure the roots went down deep and it was firmly planted.

"There were lots of people who were sure it was going to wither and die. This wasn't its natural home and it had already been moved once, but McRae was right. It's been several years now and the sequoia is growing well. I saw it the other day. Hycroft's grounds and gardens are among the most beautiful in Vancouver and nothing crowns them better than that tree sitting there on the top of the crest."

(Pioneer Charlie Major died long ago, as have all the people who were involved with moving McRae's tree. The Major estate is now the built-up, busy area around Sixth Street and Fifth Avenue in today's New Westminster.)

Maillardville:
French Canadians Arrive

The *Vancouver Daily Province* newspaper in 1907 announced that a new millionaire had arrived in Vancouver ready to spend money on development. McRae had been in and out of the city several times but now he was ready to become a part of the west coast scene. He was to be the man in the limelight for any new ventures undertaken in the area by Davidson or McRae. It wasn't long before a B.C. magazine article described McRae's partner Davidson as the "best class of Canadian businessman" and it credited him with great foresight and force of character. The periodical said he was the most likeable of men and it also noted that McRae was very much a livewire. McRae wanted to be recognized as an investor and a man with business acumen and influence as quickly as possible.

Andrew Davidson worked with McRae in B.C. for the first few years, but he never established a permanent home in Canada, claiming that because he was over 50 it was too late for him to move. He retained his permanent residence in Duluth, but constantly travelled between Vancouver, Winnipeg, Toronto, Ottawa, and Minneapolis with frequent trips to Britain and Europe. He still had interests in Minnesota and Winnipeg and was actively involved as a director in a long list of companies, such as the Canadian Northern Railway.

The prairie settlement project had been a wonderful money-maker from the beginning. While it would contribute to the wealth of the Davidsons and McRae for years to come, the fun of bringing the whole thing together and making it work was over. In a pattern that was becoming characteristic of him, McRae went in search of new challenges. With his move to B.C. he became an inactive partner in the affairs of Davidson and McRae Ltd. in Winnipeg; although, he still held shares in the firm. Colonel Davidson remained president and the agency's day-to-day operation was in the capable hands of Alexander Davidson who managed Davidson and McRae Limited until the Canadian Northern Railway was sold in 1918.

As the close-knit family of Davidsons and McRaes reshuffled their responsibilities, they met in Duluth to celebrate a happy family occasion: the marriage of Colonel Andrew Davidson's daughter Edith to Thomas S. Darling, a native of New York, which took place on July 11, 1907. Davidson maintained what was referred to in newspaper reports as a magnificent home at 1525 East Superior Street where the wedding took place, being "one of the most notable functions in the social history of Duluth." The young couple was expected to take up residence in Winnipeg before the winter was over where Thomas would begin working for Davidson and McRae Limited under the direction of his new uncle Alexander Davidson.

Unlike Davidson, McRae had decided to put down roots in Vancouver and become a part of this bustling young Canadian city where he felt anything was possible, especially for someone with a bit of money. He immediately applied for membership in the Vancouver Club. His objective was to invest as close to home as possible in industries that would sustain him and his family for years into the future. While he dealt with architects, contractors, and landscape artists who were building his palatial home in Shaughnessy, he also studied the business and investment scene, looking for areas he believed were ripe for development.

The shortage of lumber for building on the prairies had first drawn McRae to the Pacific coast and this was one of the reasons he had visited Vancouver and taken a look at the vast forests and countless saw-milling operations in the province. Here was the raw material to supply the prairie market and more. B.C.

was also rich in minerals, and he thought the fishing industry might have some potential.

By the time McRae's family moved to Vancouver he had already made several investments, one in Canadian North Pacific Fisheries; although, he claimed fishing was always a gamble. The first year the company made a half million dollars and the following year it failed. He lost everything he had put into it. Not an auspicious beginning, but another fishing venture fared better, and he told friends that Wallace Fisheries was better managed, and more tightly controlled. He was then president of the operation and had used his particular talent for organization to advantage.

McRae had also studied the operation of the larger sawmills in the province and found one which he felt had great potential, but it had a transportation problem that was killing any prospects for financial success. If he could solve that problem, the mill was big enough to supply some of the prairie demand and it could be expanded to bring profits flowing in from around the world.

After he had studied all the alternatives McRae envisioned an enormous project. It would be a huge investment, so he enlisted Davidson's assistance to create what was to become the largest lumber and wood manufacturing operation in the world at that time. The two men put together a new syndicate with Davidson as president and McRae as vice-president and general manager, and proceeded to purchase the assets of a plant on the Fraser River east of New Westminster.

The operation had been founded in 1889 by Frank Ross and James McLaren who had built the sawmill three miles upstream from New Westminster at a place they called Millside. The mill, a large one for the time, was built at a cost of $350,000. By 1891 there were 70 homes in the area, housing employees of the mill. But the company faced difficult times. The river at New Westminster was not deep and the wharf at the mill could only load large ships at high tide. When river levels were low the big ships ran aground. Also, the winters of the 1890s were unusually cold and on a number of occasions the Fraser River froze solid for several weeks, providing the unusual sight of horse-drawn sleds crossing the river. At the same time, the freeze-up halted all outbound deliveries and inbound shipments of logs from the company's four logging camps near Campbell River on Vancouver Island. The Ross-McLaren mill was soon near bankruptcy.

In March 1903 the operations were taken over by new owners from the United States—Lester David and his partner Peter Jensen, a senator from Nebraska—who renamed the company Fraser River Sawmills. The daily and seasonal problems of receiving logs and delivering goods to market continued, and despite a ready market, the mill was soon again in trouble.

When McRae found that one of the partners wanted to sell the operation he began to prepare carefully for a takeover. He recommended during a hearing into provincial forest practices in B.C. that the federal government be approached to undertake dredging the Fraser River in the interests of increasing traffic and industry all along the river to its mouth a dozen miles away in Richmond. McRae, in cooperation with a number of men who owned companies along the Fraser, prepared a joint presentation for the federal government, which was successful. Ottawa agreed to McRae's dredging proposal as far up-river as Langley. The dredging would deepen the river channel, making it possible to bring larger ships to the mill just up-river from New Westminster, and the deeper faster flowing river channel might not freeze so readily in winter. Mother Nature also co-operated for McRae, providing slightly warmer winters and less freezing on the Fraser.

With the dredging in place, McRae was ready to launch the takeover of Fraser River Sawmills. He and Davidson capitalized their new syndicate at $20 million. The investors included Sir William McKenzie and Sir Donald Mann from the Canadian Northern Railway, the Swift Brothers from the meat company in Chicago, and several English investors, among them M. Horne-Payne. Peter Jensen, one of the previous owners, continued to hold shares. The syndicate's investment facilitated the immediate reorganization and expansion of the operations, and McRae eagerly took control of the newly acquired business.

The entire plant and townsite covered 420 acres, including 80 acres of yards. The mill was a huge two-winged structure,

500 feet long, and at capacity required 1,030 men to run it; but it had been operating on a reduced shift for many years when it was purchased. With syndicate money available to him, McRae quickly upgraded old equipment and added a new shake and shingle mill adjacent to the main Fraser River mill. Fraser River Sawmills originally had 3,500 feet of deep-water frontage, but under McRae's direction this wharfing area was extended by 900 feet so that it could accommodate the larger deep-sea ships he needed for the export market. The milling operations were expanded in order to increase production. Subsidiary operations that became part of the new company included The Canadian Tugboat Company, the transportation arm of the enterprise that brought cut logs across the Strait of Georgia from Vancouver Island; and Comox Logging and Railway, also on the Island, which controlled 70,000 acres of timber located between Comox and Campbell River.

Within two years of the takeover nearly 80 percent of the mill's production was being shipped to the prairies, and 10 percent was going to Australia with another 10 percent to South Africa.

On April 25, 1910, Fraser River Sawmills had been operating under McRae's direction for more than two years when the new company was finally incorporated as Canadian Western Lumber Company. In a very short space of time McRae and Davidson would achieve remarkable success as the operation found new employees, went into round-the-clock operation, and expanded the number of its retailing centres.

In the beginning the Canadian Western Lumber Company mill employed 850 men who were paid about $2.50 per day. As demand for lumber increased on the prairies as well as abroad, shifts were added and production skyrocketed, held in check only by an absence of skilled labour. As the company prospered and gradually found the men it needed, daily wages rose to $3.50 per day.

Initially, McRae faced a severe shortage of experienced mill workers. To improve production and profits he needed more men. He sent a company representative to Quebec in search of experienced hands because he had read of some discontent in the mills there. In the major lumbering towns of Rockland, Ontario and Hull, Quebec, 60 or 70 men were persuaded to travel to the west coast, providing their fare was paid. Some of them, however, were drifters who took advantage of the offer of free travel and then disappeared shortly after their arrival.

McRae still needed employees and was reluctant to hire large numbers of available Asians because of the friction it might cause in the mill and the community where everyone lived. The race riots of 1907 in Vancouver were still fresh in the minds of many people and the deep-seated racial prejudice against Orientals had not abated. Many immigrants from Scotland had threatened to walk out of operations that employed Orientals. The Chinese were eager to work; but, McRae wanted a trouble-free majority white work force if he could find one.

Andrew Davidson suggested McRae talk to the local Roman Catholic priest, Father William O'Boyle, about getting French Canadian families rather than single men to come west. He also recommended that a land grant be a part of the offer made to new employees, providing they were experienced milling men. The priest whole-heartedly agreed that the introduction of French Canadian families would provide a stable work force and would be an answer to the Oriental labour question. It would also expand the number of Roman Catholics in the area and improve the church's influence. O'Boyle offered to make the trip to Quebec himself to find families who would consider relocating to a new community on the Fraser River where they would be offered steady employment, land on which to build their homes, and lumber with which to build them.

On September 26, 1909, the first French Canadian families, totalling 140 people, travelled on a special train from the St. Francis Valley in Quebec across thousands of miles by rail to the far Pacific coast to find better wages and a better life for their families. It was a new start for many of them. All had agreed to the simple contract with the company, which stated that for $150 the company would sell them a half acre of land on which to build a house, would also furnish lumber and paint, and provide a salary to men of working age. In most instances, land and building supplies came to a total cost of less than $1,000. They would pay for materials through a monthly deduction that amounted to between $5 and $10 per month.

All went well for the new settlers, and the following year Father O'Boyle set out again and returned on June 7, 1910 with five coaches full of French Canadians—a total of 166 people. Nearly all of the newcomers were in family groups, the largest a group of twelve. The most common name among the newcomers was Pare; there were 31 of them. Today there are 50 families named Pare listed in the Greater Vancouver phone book, with most of them living in the Coquitlam-Maillardville area; the total number of family members is difficult to guess.

Albert Beaulieu, who became one of the leaders of the new community in 1912, explained the details of the agreement he had made with the company before moving west. He had arrived in the aforementioned group of twelve and now they were thirteen. He had eleven children, so his requirements were considerable. He noted, "We have 85 families and our population is nearly 500. You see we are prosperous here and if the little ones come they are welcome."

In the short time since he had arrived in 1909 Beaulieu had built an eight-room home and had been offered $3,000 for it. He refused to sell and commented, "In a little while we will have electric lights and other conveniences, just as many of us now have the telephone." Summing up his situation, Beaulieu said, "Personally I could not be better situated. In my employment with the company I am earning four dollars a day out of which I am only paying back to the company eight dollars a month on my property." When he settled in the community he had no property at all and now estimated what he owned at $5,000.

In 1912, Father O'Boyle said to a visiting dignitary, "My present conviction is now, as it was when the colony was started, that colonizing the country with such settlers, as the French-Canadians or other natives of Eastern Canada is the best and surest way of solving the problem of Oriental labour."

The new village that grew on Coquitlam Road was on the northern boundary of the lumber company's townsite and was adjacent to what was known as the "White City," because all the houses were painted white. This unorganized municipality was set aside for the exclusive use of Caucasians employed at the mill who rented the houses for a fee of $5 to $16 dollars per month, depending on their needs and the size of their families. It was an attractive community with direct streetcar transportation into New Westminster and was furnished with its own post office, general store, butcher shop, restaurant, barbershop, and ice cream parlour. It also contained a baseball field, tennis courts, and a ballroom where dances were held each Saturday night. If a man left the mill, he also gave up his housing in the White City.

In the French-Canadian colony the arrangement was different. So long as the occupant paid the required instalments he remained in possession of his house. He was the purchaser of the property, and although morally obligated to the company, the property was his to retain or sell as he chose.

The French Canadians brought their Quebec lifestyle with them and had soon built brightly coloured homes that dominated the village. One visitor described the setting: "An extraordinary panorama opened up before me. Nestling close to the base of the hill was a group of brightly painted ornamentally be-balconied houses. High above the others stood another structure, surmounted by a cross." One of the first community structures completed by the new French Canadian residents was the church at the end of their main street. A residence was also built for the priest and a convent for nuns, The Sisters of Child Jesus, who came to teach the rapidly growing number of children. The church cost $7,000 to build and seated 300 people while the house and convent were built for $4,000. Canadian Western Lumber Company donated the land. This part of the village was later named Maillardville, after the priest, Father Edmond Maillard, oblate of Mary Immaculate, who was the founding pastor of the parish of Notre Dame de Lourdes. The community grew quickly and soon became the largest French Canadian settlement west of Quebec.

The brightly coloured houses of the French Canadians soon dominated the company town that before long was named Maillardville—after the village priest, Father Edmond Maillard. Today it remains true to its French Canadian name and heritage as a well-recognized French-speaking suburb of Vancouver, and a part of the broader Coquitlam community.

Despite his stated aversion to the problem presented by Oriental labour, McRae gradually accommodated a mulitcultural work force. Regardless of his personal bias, McRae's housing policy stated that when not working, employees of any religious faith were free to pursue their particular ceremonies without molestation. There were in 1912 almost 100 Chinese and Japanese employed by the company in addition to over 200 East Indians, who lived in red houses to the east of the French Canadian village. These homes were described as low structures appropriate for the needs of a large number of single men. Father O'Boyle once said the interiors were clean although not to be compared with the immaculate Japanese quarters. McRae had insisted that the company take all possible precautions to reduce racial tension by giving the Hindus their own part of the settlement as had been done for the Chinese, Japanese, and Greeks. McRae tried to be fair in all his dealings with his employees.

In the centre of the East Indian settlement was a store where the common practice of trading in goods took place. A Hindu who rented the building from the company managed the store. To the east of the store was a temple where at almost any hour of the day or evening shoes would be placed outside the door and a number of worshippers could be seen crouching on the floor. "The routine of their lives varies but little from that of their lighter skinned neighbours," was a comment attributed to the mill manager.

The East Indians had, however, required more accommodation than any of the other groups because of their "uncanny burial practices" and "occasional devil chasing." On one occasion this practice proved to be of some interest to the whole community although somewhat frustrating to the participants. It revolved around a custom that was necessary whenever the holy book was moved from one place to another. On this particular occasion it was a trying task, due to the stubborn refusal of the "Evil One" to permit the procession of people to go about their devotions unmolested. As described in the *Victoria Daily Colonist* newspaper, "it took the faithful fully ten days to get their sacred book past the lumber company's waste burner. The procession started time and again, but despite the fact that the priest castigated the air violently with his switch, very little progress could be made. The 'Demon of Darkness' refused to budge. On the 10th day by indefatigably lashing the atmosphere, and by vociferous chanting, which attracted many mystified Caucasian spectators, the 'Plutonian obstructionist' was routed, and the procession resolved into a foot race which carried the worshippers well through the White City to the eastern limits of New Westminster. From there the march proceeded more sedately and the 'Holy Word' was carried in triumph into the city beyond." All hoped that the book would not require another move in the near future.

When the new company was incorporated in 1910 the tally for the Fraser Mills townsite listed 499 homes built or under construction, 79 single boarders at the hotel, and 20 single boarders at the company clubhouse. Among the inhabitants were 12 Greeks, 5 Norwegians, 66 Japanese, 24 Chinese, and 172 Hindus. There was a list of lost arrivals—men who quit, departed, or for a variety of reasons were let go. The census ended with the line: "Total White Men, 615, with a grand total of 943."

The expansion of the mill, the arrival of the French Canadians, and the almost immediate success of the new company completely changed the character and prosperity of the community. The number of employees soared to over 2,000 as the mills operated around the clock. In a public statement some years later, McRae announced that the company had paid out $19 million in wages and had purchased equipment and supplies worth $15 million.

In 1912 a feature story about Canadian Western Lumber Company appeared in the *Daily Colonist* that began, "The extraordinary virility of enterprise, breadth of vision and daring which is making Canada the new Land of Promise, finds its highest typification, perhaps, in the business institution which the Canadian Western Lumber Company has created at Fraser Mills." The unnamed reporter may have exaggerated; but, there is no question he was impressed with McRae's achievements, describing the operation as one of the finest examples of colonization and one of the cleanest and sanest partnerships between labour and capital to be found anywhere in the western hemisphere.

The reporter said the mill annually produced enough lumber, linearly measured, to more than cover the earth's circumference or to build a small city. He described the scene he visited: "Between the picturesque French Canadian colony on the north and the southeastern outpost where the swarthy disciples of Guru Nanak intermittently chant beside their funeral pyres, the most absorbing phase of this giant plant is its polyglot of peoples and the intimate, human note which pervades every branch of the establishment."

The *Daily Colonist* sent its reporter to view the mill's operations. His story gives a layman's view of the gigantic production facility that came into being under the direction of Alexander McRae. He obviously found this new-generation, highly mechanized mill fascinating and waxed almost poetic in his description of it.

First to the long pond where the marked monarchs take their first step in the process of being reincarnated into useful articles of commerce. Standing at the base of a long incline called the slip were two men with pike poles who shoved the logs upon the incline chain. Intersecting this chain, at intervals, were sharp teethed, uncomfortable-looking objects called saddles and once the log was securely seated on one of these its journey was short and its dismemberment incredibly swift. Reaching the summit of the incline, the log continues through the grooved channel until it reaches the particular rig or band saw for which it is intended. The marvelous power of modern machinery is epitomized when darting up swiftly from underneath the floor, three notched steel bars suddenly smash their way into the side of a log and send it crashing to one side. Some of these forest monarchs are 110 feet in length and nine feet in diameter.

There are three of these rigs that for twenty hours out of twenty-four, six days of the week, year in and year out ceaselessly slice off timbers as easily as the ordinary knife cuts through cheese. Men working swiftly on the various carriages manipulate huge hooks in the meantime to hold the wood giants in place while others by simply twisting a crank regulate the depth of each slice, as ordered by the sawyer. ...

[It's] a miracle-working home of wonder-working machinery where one great 65-bladed affair working perpendicularly pares off more than half a hundred planks at the same time. Another is a saw working up from the floor, which halts some of the passing produce long enough to shear off the ends and then sinks swiftly back under the floor again as if with the consciousness of duty well done.

There is a man sitting at an arrangement generally described as a piano. Running forward and upward from the keys in front of the operator, a large number of wires connect with a vertical flock of saws working downward from the roof. These whirling discs work in doubles, trebles, quartettes, in sixes or in half a dozen other combinations at the direction of the man at the keys. They are called trimmers. The man looks down on the steady stream of timber and decides how they ought to be cut, his decision swayed by the necessity of getting as much as possible out of every stick or plank. His judgment, wherein lies his value, must be instantaneous, for there is little time, and as he decides the discs keep rising and falling, very much like a flock of rubber balls playing in so many fountains.

Typical of this era, the main conveyor belt for the mill was made of leather; the one at McRae's sawmill had been made from the hides of 72 steers. The sheer magnitude of the plant and the enormous scale upon which it carried on its various activities were unheard of anywhere else on the coast at this time and impressed all who saw it. The mill was equipped with ten kilns, capable of raising the temperature to 300 degrees so the wood could be dried in 24 hours and quickly made into dry planks ready for the planing mill. This drying process was faster than any other mill on the coast; some took two to three times as long to dry their wood.

McRae was proud of the fact that the mill processed a log a minute and there was not another plant anywhere in the country that did as well. Normal capacity was 750 thousand feet of lumber a day. However, in one stretch from August 1 to September 22, 1912 the mill claimed production of 100 million feet of lumber. By the year end the mill had cut 175 million feet. It produced enough lumber each day to fill 42 cars and had yard facilities for loading 130 at a time. Stockpiled in the yard in September 1912 were 42 million feet of lumber with ten million in sheds and the rest in piles in the yard, all of it destined for market. The mill was at this time shipping out everything it could produce. Even working night and day it could not begin to meet demand.

Once again Alexander McRae's business acumen was proven. He had been the right man in the right place at the right time. He said he always invested his own money in ventures that interested him and stayed with them to the end. Of his investments in B.C. he claimed about 90 percent were successful and only 10 percent failed. By 1914 he was president of the Anacortes Lumber and Box Company; vice-president of Columbia River Lumber Company Ltd. of Golden, which became a subsidiary of Canadian Western; vice-president of Canadian Collieries (Dunsmuir) Ltd. of Victoria; and president of Wallace Fisheries.

McRae retained an active interest in the operations of Western Canadian Lumber Company only until 1914, when he left the mills in the capable hands of Andrew Davidson and the men he had hired to run them. It was the beginning of the First World War and Ottawa called on McRae to help organize the Canadian army into an efficient fighting force.

When war was declared in 1914, McRae (now in the army) and Davidson were both in London, and together they went to meet the first Canadian troops as they arrived in Liverpool. It was a proud moment for both of them; unfortunately it would be McRae's final cherished memory of his dear friend, cousin, and business associate. McRae had no way of knowing that as he said goodbye to Andrew it would end the nearly twenty years they had spent in business together. Andrew Davidson died in the Mayo Clinic in Rochester, Minnesota in the fall of 1916 at the age of 62. The holdings of the Davidsons and McRae then became the responsibility of Alexander Davidson who held the reins on his own until the war ended in 1918 and McRae returned home.

Major General
the Honourable Sam Hughes

When the First World War began in Europe, Canadians immediately wanted to do everything possible to support Great Britain in its conflict with the Kaiser, but the young Dominion was largely unprepared. Many recent immigrants returned to the land of their birth for the duration. One man who had anticipated the war was Major General Sam Hughes who in 1912 began to bolster the number of men in the militia. Major General Hughes explained to his colleagues the positions he held and why he sought out Alexander McRae. He had in mind a specific position, a key role for the man from Hycroft.

I know some critics mocked my entry in the Parliamentary Guide, probably the longest in the book in 1916, a year which was to become a milestone marker of my life. What was different about my entry and those of most of my political colleagues was that I had a proud story to tell of my family's military history, and of my own solid background and record of achievement despite what latterly was stated and written of me. The critics, my political foes, the backbiters and the envious have called me eccentric, some even said mad, charming, egomaniac, tyrant, brusque, anti-French Canadian, meddler, bungler in military matters, unfair critic of British generals in their handling of the war in France in 1914-16 with disastrous results and the deaths of many Canadian soldiers, and much more. I have made my case. I leave the verdict to history. I have no fear of what it will say.

As the Parliamentary Guide stated, I was born in Darlington, Ontario, in 1853 of Scottish, Irish and Huguenot ancestors. My known military history goes back to my great grandfather who served under Napoleon. I studied at University of Toronto, lectured at Toronto College Institute, and bought The Lindsay Warder newspaper which I edited until 1897. I was first elected to Ottawa in 1891 as the Member of Parliament for the riding of Victoria and Haliburton, and I had the honour to sit in the House of Commons for 30 years secure in the trust of the voters who returned me seven times.

Early in my life I became convinced that the militia was vital to the interests of Canada not only in the matter of defense, but essential in the lives of communities across the country and in the up-bringing of the young men of Canada. As I have stated, the Canadian militia upholds manhood, defends homes and loved ones, supplies teachers and instructors all over Canada for the cadet corps, Boy Scouts, physical training, training of school teachers, schools of military instruction and at times police; upholds youth, mentally, morally, physically, instills the spirit of obedience, discipline, patriotism, veneration and love for principle; preserves the spirit for liberty and independence and keeps the old flag flying to the breezes and trains boys to be an asset to the nation.

I served in the militia during the Fenian raids in 1870 when I was very young. I saw the value of the force to Canada and I worked my way up through the ranks becoming a lieutenant-colonel in the 45th Battalion. I was a staunch believer in the British

Empire but I saw Canada as an equal partner, not subservient and answerable in all things to Great Britain. I strongly advocated colonial military assistance in imperial wars in Egypt, Sudan, Afghanistan and South Africa and offered to personally raise Canadian corps. In 1897 after going to London for the Diamond Jubilee of Queen Victoria, I even traveled to Australia and New Zealand to try to win their support in such participation. I went to South Africa during the Boer war and was mentioned in dispatches several times.

My political career was marked in 1911 by my appointment as Minister of Militia and it was through my efforts in this role that I came into contact with Alexander Duncan McRae. I feared war was coming in Europe and I wanted to increase the strength and efficiency of the militia, to be ready for the fight because Canada would battle at Britain's side without question. The officer ranks badly needed men with experience. There were some in place who were devoted to the cause, but, I must admit, there were those who preferred to swank about armories wearing uniforms and swords, eager enthusiasts of formal mess dinners and military balls. Military training and preparedness were secondary.

I clashed with the senior officers of the small, regular Canadian army, which I felt looked down on the militia while itself being sadly organized and inefficient. I firmly believed that the men of the militia would be the backbone of the Canadian corps in the upcoming struggle. To heighten its performance I needed more men of various capabilities and experience. I traveled the country from coast-to-coast to find those of the calibre that I wanted. On the Pacific coast I was told of McRae, a man with great organizational skills who had been a prime mover in the colonization of Saskatchewan some ten years before. He then headed a vast industrial complex in British Columbia, including the biggest sawmill in the world and extensive fishing and mining interests. McRae was approached, told of the importance and urgency of the matter, and urged to be part of the militia. With some persuasion he finally agreed, I am glad to say, and the record shows significantly and impressively, that I made a very astute and wise choice. His work as quartermaster general of the troops overseas was outstanding.

As is well known, I was promoted to the rank of major general in 1914, and received the KCB from King George after one of my many visits to the frontlines in France. From the beginning it was obvious that McRae was doing a first-class job. This led to his promotion and eventually his responsibility for vital supplies and their smooth movement to the troops in France, a highly involved process that he handled splendidly despite many problems both from fellow Canadians and from our allies. It has been well publicized that I clashed with the British senior military men for their handling of the war in the early years which I believed was horrendous and caused many young Canadian lives to be lost unnecessarily. I also challenged their political leaders, who would not hear of any criticism of the military wisdom of their generals. They said I knew nothing whatsoever about the conduct of battles and campaigns. They charged that I exaggerated my own achievements, and made many bad mistakes in procurement in which I tried to use Canadian designed and manufactured equipment which they contended was not up to par. This included the much-criticized Ross rifle which they said was too heavy, too prone to jamming in the mud of the trenches and was much hated by our own troops.

The rows with the British also increased my arguments and disagreements with some of our own senior officers and with the politicians at home. The upshot was that in 1916 I was fired from my job and my military role, in effect, was over. I have refuted the charges and criticisms hurled against me and defended my policies and positions. One that remains unsullied is the build up I created in the militia prior to 1914, without which our army would have been desperately short of men in the early days, and my recruitment of men such as Alexander Duncan McRae, whose achievements and service to Canada are already enshrined in our country's history books.

Never a Shot in Anger

McRae took his role as a militia officer seriously although he knew a military career would never be for him because he preferred to give orders rather than take them. In 1912 he began as a Hughes' recruit with the rank of honorary lieutenant colonel, and wound up the war in 1918 as a major general. McRae was persuaded to join the Duke of Connaught's Own Rifles in Vancouver. While not a vain man, a picture taken outside an armory along with his fellow officers shows McRae quite pleased to don the dashing uniform and stand with hand on sword.

In 1914 he was 40 years of age. His army career was highlighted by his many accomplishments in the role he was ordered to fill. His foes in later political battles attacked him as a soldier who never heard a shot fired in anger, a rich man who found himself a cushy, safe billet in which to spend the First World War while garnering acclaim. The accusations were unfair and untrue, primarily politically motivated. McRae's talents were used in a job where he excelled—as organizer, procurer, facilitator, and as a man who honed efficiency to its sharpest edge. He made many trips to France to check on conditions in the trenches, to see if provisions were reaching their destination and if the lines of communication were open. A crumbling piece of paper among his army records held at the National Archives in Ottawa confirms only one of these trips, a special duty that departed on June 4, 1916. He was in France on this occasion for a week.

When the war broke out in August 1914, McRae and Davidson were in England making some final business arrangements before the anticipated outbreak of war. They were both on hand with Sam Hughes to greet the first Canadian troops to arrive before they crossed the channel to the killing fields of Belgium and France. Returning to Canada, McRae immediately enlisted with the Canadian Army Service Corps. His service number was 34302. The next month Hughes appointed McRae to head remount operations in western Canada, where he was responsible for purchasing horses for the army. It was a department that had become severely dysfunctional, plagued with rumours of wartime profiteering, financial kickbacks, and bribery. Among the malfeasance discovered were inflated veterinary bills, sometimes for services never performed, and charges for livestock feed that were never delivered. Local committees formed to make the purchases were based on patronage and political appointments. Reorganization of the system was essential, and in short order McRae identified procedures that were driving up costs, brought in his own auditor, and ordered the removal of various committee members.

McRae totally reorganized the Remount Commission in the west and was responsible for the purchase of some 8,000 horses for the army, but rumours of fraud and skullduggery in the nation-wide program continued and became so intense that the federal government ordered a royal commission to probe the charges. Not only did Royal Commissioner Sir Charles Peers Davidson clear McRae of any suggestion of wrongdoing, but he commended him very favourably for his performance. The problems were all elsewhere in the system.

Hughes appointed McRae a full lieutenant colonel on May 11, 1915, and the man from Hycroft went overseas with the Second Canadian Division. Within two months, on July 15, he was promoted to the post of overseas director of supplies and transport. McRae's business acumen and organizational skills had become abundantly apparent and he was given control of purchases, distribution of supplies, transportation of troops and the wounded between England and France, and in addition, was in charge of training reinforcements for the front.

Support for Hughes waned as he continued his unswerving support of the Canadian designed and manufactured Ross rifle. Reports came back of soldiers ditching the weapon as soon as they could in favour of the British Lee Enfield. McRae heard the complaints and had the Ross re-chambered for the Second Division before these men left for the front. While it improved the weapon, the Ross rifle continued to be controversial, even becoming a political issue, and was never considered a suitable weapon for the Canadian infantry.

McRae set about applying the business practices he had honed in British Columbia to the Canadian military in order to affect savings and improve performance. He found the existing system plagued with chaos and confusion. Ordering supplies was erratic and uneven, and records showed a litany of scarcity for some troops and an over abundance for others. McRae tackled the problems on a broad front. He investigated the food served to the men, beginning with the quality purchased to the way it was prepared and finally cooked. Army "grub" has been a target for soldiers' complaints and grousing since Caesar's legions crossed the Alps, and probably before, but McRae sought improvements. He had new food standards set based on the dietary findings of the times. Following tradition, troops continued to find fault, although objective opinion confirmed the daily rations were much better than they had been previously. In addition, McRae's innovations cut costs by a million dollars in one year.

McRae's military career was under review after Hughes was fired in 1916, but only because he was a Hughes appointment. There was more than a little backbiting in the senior ranks of the Canadian army, and some of the former minister's appointments were viewed as his favourites and were only there on his sufferance. There were those who were not up to par and were cut down, but McRae found satisfaction in the fact that he was not one of them. His run up the ladder was based on performance, not favouritism.

His duties overseas kept him busier than ever before and perhaps that was fortunate for it left little time for him to grieve.

Early in 1916, he learned that his cousin and mentor, his friend and business partner from the beginning had taken ill. Davidson's condition worsened and he was taken to the Mayo Clinic, but nothing could be done for him and he died there on April 22, 1916. The two men had worked together for twenty years. The man was much more like an older brother than a cousin to McRae, and the adventures and memories they shared were the best of a lifetime. McRae could never have achieved such great success so early in life without the patronage of this congenial, talented man and he knew he would never again know the camaraderie, excitement, and sense of accomplishment he and Andrew had enjoyed together. He would never forget the thrill he felt during those train trips across the prairies, each car

By 1917, McRae was a quartermaster general and received the Order of the Bath for outstanding performance overseas. By the end of the year he was promoted to the rank of brigadier general, and finally to temporary major general, when he undertook the task of setting up the first Ministry of Information for Great Britain.

filled with millionaires ready to purchase land in the Canadian territory, or the pride he and Davidson shared in developing the biggest forest products company on the continent and making it profitable.

McRae's career continued to soar, and on December 4, 1916 he was promoted to the post of quarter master general overseas.

He knew Davidson would have been proud of his new appointment.

McRae's reorganization of supply and services continued. In February 1917, he saved Canadians almost a half-million dollars by getting exemption from a British excise tax on goods brought in for Canadians. Despite the fact that Canada was an ally, helping to fight the war, the British had imposed the tax that might have remained in effect had McRae not argued them out of it. He produced better results for less in hospital costs and his constant improvements in supplies and standards produced further savings in food expenditures. Mindful of every nickel, McRae even saved money by switching military policemen from horseback to bicycles, although the new saddles did not sit well with them.

McRae's outstanding performance overseas earned him the Order of the Bath in June 1917. His military record shows that during the next month his service was further noticed when it was formally brought to the attention of the Secretary of State, a non-medal form of recognition. In December that year he was promoted again, this time to the rank of brigadier general. It has been suggested that McRae was offered a knighthood by the British government, pushed by Lord Beaverbrook, who was born a Canadian in New Brunswick but was at this time an English lord and an influential cabinet minister at Westminster. McRae supposedly turned down the offer of a title although he never confirmed or denied the story that it was actually made.

McRae's friendship with Lord Beaverbrook was also one of the reasons for a request from British Prime Minister Lloyd George, who in February 1918 asked that McRae be loaned to Britain to establish the country's first Ministry of Information. This was an unprecedented request; British politicians must have been exceedingly impressed with McRae's recent performance and organizational ability to ask for his services rather than calling on a British resident. There is no doubt they were also well aware of his promotional and advertising successes on the prairies with the Saskatchewan Valley Land Company for it was this experience they wanted to duplicate for the new ministry. McRae was promoted to the rank of temporary major general in order to take on this important role. It was the kind of project McRae loved to tackle: something new that he could organize in his own way and know, when he was finished, that there were few who could have done the job better. Lord Beaverbrook, who was to become Britain's first minister of information, undoubtedly appreciated McRae's talents as well. For his part, McRae's experience with the new Ministry of Information taught him more tricks of the trade that he would later put to use—with varying results —in his political career.

McRae's military career ended when he was mustered out in December 1918, a month after war's end. His records in the National Archives show he received a war service gratuity of $575—hardly a week's pocket money for the Vancouver millionaire although he had earned it like all the others. His pay in 1917 was $650 a month, including a London living allowance. His wife, Blaunche, received a $60 a month separation allowance.

Despite his outstanding performance and the success of his endeavours in the army, McRae's wartime record was frequently criticized, probably only because his next foray took him into the field of politics. One political opponent called him a mere "tin-hat soldier," which wasn't even a proper insult. A tin-hat soldier usually meant one who was in action;

McRae's contributions to the war effort and his performance for the British government eventually brought him recognition there. He was presented at the court of King George VI at Buckingham Palace in the late 1930s.

the critic likely meant a "brass-hat soldier," meaning he was one of the brass but had not earned the rank in action. McRae took little interest in the military after the war as he moved on to new adventures; however, he did speak out on several occasions in support of the needs of returning veterans, particularly the wounded. For unknown reasons he wasn't called on to serve his country in any meaningful way in 1939 when the Second World War erupted. At the age of 55 he was still capable of performing an important role and he had lost none of his abilities to organize large projects and bring them through to fruition, but it wasn't to be.

McRae's Provincial Party

At the outbreak of the war in 1914 McRae had removed himself from direct control of the many parts of his industrial empire; so, at the age of 45 and newly discharged, he began to look for new interests to occupy his mind. The old operations were running well without his active support. He had all the money he needed, but he was too energetic and too interested in the world around him to spend the rest of his life on the sidelines. On February 6, 1919 the *Vancouver Sun* printed a tribute to his contributions during the war, saying that "his services to the Canadian West have been of the greatest value and it is not too much to say that the work of he and his colleagues achieved more practical results of a higher order than the scheming of a generation of politicians has produced." This was an unusually generous salute from a rabidly Liberal paper to a well-known millionaire Conservative.

In the next three or four years McRae took a look at several new business enterprises with his usual attention to the natural resource sectors. At the same time, his age, his experience, the glowing reports of his service during the war, and his great wealth resulted in a number of requests for speaking engagements. While he knew he was no silver-tongued orator, he was knowledgeable on a number of subjects and he spoke to various gatherings in B.C., in other parts of Canada, and in the United States. These talks usually addressed business groups and large organizations for he had a wealth of information that was much in demand. He spoke at home on the need for Canadian post-war reconstruction and the need for the country to provide "every man with a responsible opportunity for a job." He opposed the concept of a welfare state, but he held the view that the state did have a responsibility to ensure that people had opportunities to provide for themselves. He was particularly concerned with the future of war veterans, who soon after the last gun roared, began to complain about the treatment they were accorded by a seemingly unfeeling and unfair government. They were unhappy with politicians who had hailed them in war but now ignored them in peace. McRae, the former general, called on the government to accommodate them, particularly those who had come home with serious wounds and disabilities. He was not in step with many Tories when he also called for a major increase in public works across Canada, including the building of a St. Lawrence River canal, in order to help provide jobs for veterans and the unemployed.

One of McRae's favourite topics in B.C. was the future development of his province, the place he had chosen to make his home. From the very first he believed there was a great untapped potential in the development of the Peace River country, which he saw as a great benefit to Alberta, B.C., and the whole of Canada. His ideas were slightly ahead of the times, but were eventually carried out at a later date by a B.C. premier, W.A.C. Bennett, who did not arrive on the political scene until after McRae's demise. McRae also often voiced the view that Canada needed many more people of the right stock, preferably from Britain (like the ones that had first come to Saskatchewan) who would move as homesteaders into the Peace River country.

McRae's speeches also stressed that there should be a drive to expand Canada's foreign trade, while maintaining a measure of protection for homemade products. He confidently predicted that if these and other expansion policies were put in place, they would be well worth the initial investment, and the development they produced would give Canada a population of 25 million people by 1950. The projects he espoused did not come to pass nor did the population increase as he predicted. Canada had less than fifteen million residents by the middle of the twentieth century, and 35 million by 2001.

Before civic audiences in Vancouver McRae gradually became a critic of the B.C. political scene. His expertise in the efficient financing of large organizations made it impossible for him not to find fault with the way the provincial government was spending funds. He thought both the Liberal and Conservative governments of the day were guilty of throwing away money given to them by the taxpayers, and he was quite blunt in his accusations. He was particularly angry at the saga of the Pacific Great Eastern Railway (PGE), whose turbulent and costly history plagued the province for more than four decades. When the line from Vancouver to the northern Interior was first proposed in 1910, it was to run 450 miles to Prince George and be finished by 1915. This wasn't achieved until 1956 despite major infusions of public money and much angry debate.

McRae's outspoken criticism of the B.C. situation didn't sit well with fellow Conservatives, who had relinquished power in 1916 when the government of W.J. Bowser lost to Liberal John Oliver in a nasty election campaign, rancorous even by B.C.'s hellfire standards. It was reported that McRae wanted to run for the Tories in the 1920 provincial election but was talked out of it by Bowser, who felt McRae's criticism of the party and his own leadership had been too strong, and perhaps too close to the mark for comfort. The electors again returned Oliver's administration but were almost immediately unhappy with what they had done. There was great dissatisfaction with both major parties as the post-war provincial economy began to stagnate, resulting in high unemployment. The mounting unrest crossed both Liberal and Conservative Party lines, and before the next election the majority was calling for a clean-sweep. Critics voiced their unhappiness with the slogan, "Get Oliver out and don't let Bowser in." More and more residents began to believe, as McRae did, that political bungling and incompetence was squandering the province's opportunities for progress. Voices became louder, demanding change and suggesting that it was time for old-party ties to be broken in favour of something new.

At the Vancouver Club McRae discussed with his colleagues the options open to them for improving the province's economic performance and getting it back on a sound footing. Many of them felt as he did that the critics were right and a new alternative must be found.

In the midst of these discussions, in the spring of 1922, the McRae family was suddenly called to Minneapolis, to the bedside of Mama Howe, Blaunche's mother, who had taken seriously ill. While visiting his mother-in-law, whose health soon began to improve, McRae spent some time thinking about the situation back home and making some decisions about his own future aspirations.

But first he encouraged his oldest daughter Blanche to make a decision of her own. She had become engaged to Richard Plunkett Baker, nephew of the wealthy Mrs. Lily Lefevre, who sat on the board of several large Vancouver companies and was recognized for the poetry she wrote; but the Bakers and Lefevres were Roman Catholics while the McRaes were Presbyterians. The wedding had been postponed once because of this religious conflict, but McRae asked his daughter to make a decision now and suggested that if she chose to marry Richard in a Roman Catholic ceremony, meaning their children would all be brought up as Catholics, the wedding should take place while the family was in Minneapolis, away from Vancouver and the gossip that would ensue if she were married at home. Richard had refused to be married in a Presbyterian Church for then he would face excommunication. Blanche made her decision and married Richard, a former flying ace and member of the Royal Flying Corps who had been shot down by Baron von Richtofen, (the "Red Baron") and then held prisoner. He was a dashing war hero, a member of the Shaughnessy community, and he and Blanche made a very handsome couple.

The ceremony took place in the chapel of the Roman Catholic cathedral with members of the immediate families in attendance. Richard's mother, his aunt Mrs. Lefevre, and his sister Nano Baker travelled to Minneapolis for the ceremony, but his brother Fred was in Europe at the time and unable to make the trip across the Atlantic. All of the McRaes, including Mama Howe, attended the wedding, which was followed by a

Alexander McRae's oldest daughter Blanche McRae married Richard Baker in the chapel of the Roman Catholic Cathedral in Minneapolis, Minnesota in 1922. The young couple soon moved to their new home on Osler Avenue in Shaughnessy, just a couple of blocks from Hycroft.

small but sumptuous reception at the palatial Howe home. Blanche was the first of the McRae girls to marry and the only one to remain in Vancouver afterwards. The newlyweds, Blanche and Richard Baker, spent their honeymoon in Banff and then cruised up the Sunshine Coast before taking up residence at 3851 Osler Avenue, just a short walk from Hycroft. It was the former home of Robert Cromie, owner of the *Vancouver Sun* and was an address that before long would become quite infamous.

By the time he returned to Vancouver, McRae had decided to become more involved in trying to find a solution to the terrible political situation in B.C. He had been urged by business and professional men in both Vancouver and Victoria to put his full energy into political renewal, so he became the driving force behind the formation of a committee of 100 prominent men united in their efforts to bring about dramatic action and change.

At the same time there was another group unhappy with the old-line parties. The United Farmers of B.C. had a sound structural organization, but quickly realized they were too few in number to achieve much in politics on their own. They also favoured a restrictive, agricultural policy that wasn't going to win them many urban supporters. This was a time when more than half the population of B.C. lived within fifteen miles of Vancouver. The farmers knew they must align themselves with another group that had the city's support. As a result, when McRae funded an organizational meeting for his Committee of 100 in Vernon on January 13, 1923, the United Farmers—along with other unhappy residents—were in attendance to monitor the meeting and see what transpired. McRae's group of 100 had held an earlier meeting in Vancouver where they had drawn up a broad manifesto and were now ready to move forward.

The *Province* reported that the Provincial Party was launched towards midnight in Vernon after a day of hot discussion and debate. It said, "The United Farmers body died without suffering ... and there were no harrowing death struggles." Many members were unhappy about the demise of the organization but believed their membership would form the backbone of the new party. McRae was hailed as the new leader although he appeared reluctant to take the top post. Was he feigning or was it an emerging realization that he was more suited to behind-the-scenes organization and manoeuvring than to upfront posturing? Nonetheless, he now entered the battlefield of elected politics. He had escaped the war unscathed, but in the next seven years he would be the target of a non-stop barrage that eventually brought him defeat and severely wounded his public reputation.

McRae was well aware of the possible price he would pay, and that among his most vicious enemies would be card-carrying provincial Conservatives, some of whom were long-standing friends. He was effectively deserting them when they most needed him and his financial support. The general also knew that he was assuming a position over which he had much less control than he had insisted upon during his army career and in his business life. A consummate organizer and an analytical accountant, McRae was well liked amongst his peers; but he had never been a "glad-hander," or a man who was comfortable backslapping and kissing babies. He told the crowded Vernon hall that it was the first time he had stood on a political platform and the first party convention he had ever attended. He assured the audience that he realized it was a very serious moment. "I am undertaking a very heavy burden. I do not intend to run away from the responsibility you may choose to place upon my shoulders," he said.

He mollified the farmers by telling them, "This has been and will be a farmers' movement, and the farmers will remain a dominant factor in it." Farmers' leader John Redman was named second in command of the new Provincial Party (PP). This was McRae's first broken promise as a politician for it became quite clear in a short period of time that the business sector would run the organization, and the farmers soon drifted back to their plows. Nevertheless there was enthusiasm and hope that something new and successful had been created that would redirect B.C. politics and rejuvenate the provincial economy.

It wasn't a convention without its amusing moments. The *Province* said a Commander Lewis told the audience that the PP was a "coalition of moderately honest people determined to oust the dirty grafters at present in power." The commander obviously felt that the new group had to be only "moderately honest" to be better than the completely dishonest incumbents. A Victorian with the delightful name of Beaumont Boggs said voters should be horrified by the "want of dignity and disgraceful conduct of the members of the current House." He said the Legislature had in recent times resembled a barroom and even the presence of the first woman member, Liberal Mary Ellen Smith, who was also the first elected female legislator in the British Empire, hadn't helped the dignity or decorum of the House.

Gerry McGeer, lawyer, lifelong Liberal, future mayor of Vancouver, Member of Parliament (MP), and senator immediately sent a confidential and slashing assessment of McRae to Premier

Oliver, which presaged things to come. He wrote, "He is the brigadier general type in war, the millionaire type in times of speculation, and the great business man, all of whose investments were failures during times of peace and in times of depression he is the great reformer—the man with a remedy for all the ills of the country but who confines his remedies or limits his indications of them, to ruthless and vicious criticism and personal attacks on the men who are trying to do things." McGeer obviously knew something about ruthless and vicious attacks, as he had just mounted one against McRae and his business ventures that were untrue. The fact was that with a very few exceptions, his enterprises were successful. In the next eighteen stormy months, Oliver wove a common thread through many of his accusations against McRae and the Provincial Party. They ran back to McRae's Saskatchewan Valley Land Company days and maintained that he had made his millions too quickly for them to be completely honest and above board. His wealth, more than his politics, was hammered, and his business dealings in B.C. came under sharp attack.

The PP had its headquarters in the Imperial Chambers at the corner of Seymour and Pender Streets. It was here that the *Searchlight*, a political newspaper, was produced—all of it paid for by McRae. It was available on an irregular basis, but nine editions are contained in a bound volume in the special collections section at the Vancouver Public Library. Much of it was a rant about the PGE, and contains long lists of facts and figures. McRae claimed there were kickbacks, contracts were juggled, and patronage was common, and he recited a long litany of wrongdoing by the railway. The *Searchlight* called the project "The Great Betrayal," and it accused Premier Oliver and his predecessor, the Conservative Bowser, of having fleeced the public. McRae maintained the province's debt had climbed from $10.7 million in 1910 to $80 million in 1923. He said there were also guarantees of $20 million to the PGE, which he claimed had at the same time wasted $45 million. McRae offered to pay the costs of a special independent audit of the company's books, an offer that—naturally—was rejected by the government.

The PP quickly printed a policy statement and made it public. It contained a push for freight rate equalization by Ottawa; recommended a railway line be built to tap the wealth of the Peace River country, an unusual proposal for a provincial government; offered "the fullest measure of cooperation" with Ottawa to avoid duplication of services; suggested the gradual elimination of the Oriental labour force; the abolition of patronage; special hiring of maimed and disabled veterans; an end to personal income tax, which had been promised when it was first introduced during the First World War; and a promise to expose every piece of existing legislation "to the light of day." It was a very ambitious and idealistic policy statement and was immediately damned as outrageous, amateurish, and unworkable by the other parties.

After the PP outlined its platform, Attorney General Alex Manson, a man who was in the future to become a formidable foe, assailed McRae. In his usual arrogant style Manson said that in view of the general's business enterprises, "I am inclined to think he is hardly worth considering. We shall deal with him when the time comes."

McRae immediately reserved St. Patrick's Hall in New Westminster for 8 p.m., April 5, 1923 and challenged Manson to a debate, but the attorney general didn't show up. Instead McRae told his life story and answered any questions about his past business dealings.

To a packed audience McRae said that despite the opposition's attempts to say otherwise, he was not an American, but a Canadian, born in Ontario. "Thirty years ago when I left the farm the only place for an ambitious young man was the United States," he said, adding that after earning 50 cents a day in Glencoe he returned to Canada within a few years with $50,000 to invest. McRae stated that when he left, he took with him "at the age of eighteen the best inheritance a young man can have—a good Scottish constitution and a Presbyterian upbringing." He said Canadians often moved to the States; government figures showed some 68,000 had departed in 1922.

McRae outlined the colonization project on the prairies, which he said had brought hundreds of thousands of people to the region. He spoke of his remount project at the start of the war, stating the 8,000 horses he bought for the Canadian army cost an average $150 each after he cleaned up the purchasing system. He noted that the commissioner who probed the operation nation-wide had written, "The vigorous steps taken by Colonel McRae frustrated extensive attempts to defraud and deserves commendation."

The burning issue prior to and during the election campaign was the land speculation deal at Port Mann, conceived by the owners of the Canadian Northern Railway, McKenzie and Mann. Both Liberals and Tories attacked McRae, tying him as best they could to fast financial footwork and questionable fortune-making practices. The project had been abandoned by Canadian Northern some time earlier, and McRae's political opponents claimed that many people who invested in it lost money while McRae made it. The general explained that he was an inactive partner in the firm of Davidson–McRae Land Agents in Winnipeg, and had been inactive since 1907. This firm, however, had been the agent for the Port Mann development and many others along the rail line. He also explained that his longtime friend Andrew Davidson had been a director of the railway but had died of a serious illness in 1916. He said it was obvious that it turned out to be an "ill-timed" proposition, but he himself had never sold any Port Mann property. He added that Davidson and McRae lost money on the proposal, about a third of it his, although he did not give specific amounts. The opposition didn't relent and continued to paint him as the millionaire who profited from little people while they lost their money. Oliver later dubbed it "one of the biggest real estate swindles ever pulled off" and challenged McRae to sue, but he didn't. Despite these continuous attacks, Oliver could not provide concrete proof of the charges, even admitting in one speech that Davidson and McRae might have only been sales agents as they maintained.

Normally a private man, McRae bared his life before the audience. He said the Western Canadian Lumber Company had paid out $19 million in wages to local workers, and most of its $15 million spending on equipment and supplies benefited B.C.

He said it had been the world's largest sawmill; it had employed 2,500 workers, and even in 1923, it was operating with 1,600. McRae revealed that his shares in the company were then worth about two million dollars. He said Canadian North Pacific Fisheries had started out well, making a half-million dollars in its first year before hitting bad times and folding. He lost all his investment, but again didn't give figures. McRae allowed that Wallace Fisheries, a private company, was doing well and in the previous ten years had paid out some $4.5 million in wages and $6 million for the purchase of supplies.

McRae said his opponents had even attacked his Hycroft home, stating that it represented ostentatious spending and a lavish lifestyle. There was little doubt they were right, but McRae made no apologies. He said, "Of course my home is a bad investment— that is if any home is ever a bad investment—but the public has no cause to complain. I pay nearly $3,000 a year taxes for the privilege of having it in Vancouver and it is worth it to me. When I get through paying the butcher, the baker, and the candlestick maker and the staff of ten to twelve, which I keep around me, what I have left out of $25,000 at the end of the year would not wad a gun. Incidentally, it is a happy white man's home. No Oriental has ever been employed within its walls for one hour. That is something the politicians are not talking about. Can they say as much for themselves? Keep in mind the number I employ and the expenditures I make in the city. I think I can be given credit for supporting directly and indirectly some 50 to 60 Vancouver people. Do you think a couple of hundred such homes in Vancouver would do any harm to the people of the city or for that matter to the people of this province?"

He told the audience that one critic was having a slide prepared to flash at meetings that would show Hycroft with the message: "This is where he lives." McRae said he would have one drawn up that would state, "He didn't steal it. No! The money that built the big house came from Winnipeg too."

McRae maintained he had never sold any shares in any Canadian company in which he was not interested, and that he always had some of his own money in these ventures. Not all of it was borrowed. Of his B.C. investments, the general said about 90 percent had been successful and the other 10 percent had failed.

McRae spoke for well over an hour. He told the overflow audience, "B.C. is suffering from an extreme case of machine politics with the patronage evil carried to its fullest development." He labelled Premier Oliver the "greatest tax collector we ever had." Repeating with pride his role in the development on the prairies, he said it was a worthy story that made "a romance second not even to the Arabian nights." McRae added, "Is there today a man with red blood in his veins who can despair of the future of Canada?" The Liberal *Vancouver Sun* gave his speech extensive coverage, almost verbatim; the Tory-backed *Province* gave this presentation by a former party member—perhaps a threatening new force to the established order—short shrift with a small story tucked away inside.

To bolster his version of his career and strengthen his reply to the charges made by Oliver and other opponents, a subcommittee was set up at McRae's suggestion to check his version of his business life. It reported to the full committee in a letter, which was made public, stressing that "if it had not been for General McRae's insistence it would have considered this inquiry unnecessary and uncalled for." Signed L.G. McPhillips, the subcommittee stated: "Documentary evidence has been placed before us covering all the points made by General McRae, which has proved to our entire satisfaction that his statements are in accordance with the facts. The committee has carefully considered the various reports which have come to their ears and are satisfied that General McRae's business career and his services to his country have been of a type of which any citizen could be justly proud. Your committee, therefore, most strongly recommends that the Advisory Committee publicly reaffirm its confidence in General McRae as eminently qualified to head the Provincial Party of British Columbia."

The report was unanimously approved by the 100 members of the Advisory Committee. Oliver and the others could make their charges and voice their suspicions, but the committee was solidly behind the party leader in the belief that his account

REPORT OF SUB-COMMITTEE

The sub-committee which was appointed investigated matters very thoroughly and secured documentary evidence from unprejudiced sources covering all the statements which were made. After careful deliberation, the sub-committee returned the following report, to the Advisory Committee:

Vancouver, B. C. May 14th, 1923

To the Advisory Committee,
             Provincial Party of British Columbia

Gentlemen:

Your committee, appointed at the meeting held at 340 Cambie Street on April 12th, have made a thorough examination into the questions raised in Major-General A. D. McRae's address at New Westminster, on April 5th, pertaining to his business and public career.

Documentary evidence has been placed before them covering all the points raised by General McRae, which has proved to their entire satisfaction that his statements were in accordance with the facts. The committee has carefully considered the various rumors which have been circulated which have come to their ears, and are satisfied that General McRae's business career and his services to his country have been of a type of which any Canadian citizen could be justly proud.

Your committee, therefore, most strongly recommends that the Advisory Committee publicly reaffirm its confidence in General McRae as eminently qualified to head the organization of the Provincial Party of British Columbia.

Your committee would further state that had it not been for General McRae's personal insistence it would have considered this inquiry unnecessary and uncalled for.

Respectfully submitted,

(Signed) L. G. MCPHILLIPS, *Chairman.*

This report was submitted to the Advisory Committee, and received individual unanimous endorsement from them.

PROVINCIAL PARTY OF BRITISH COLUMBIA

ADVISORY COMMITTEE

Abbott, J.L.G.	Dockrill, Col.W.	Leckie, Col. J.E.	Robertson, Robert
Allan, John W.	Ewing, Dr. Francis	Leckie, Wm.	Rolston, Frank J.
Allan, O. B.	Evans, Walter F.	Leith, David	Rorison, Col. W. D.
Alley, F. R.	Forsythe, George S.	Leveson, E.J.	Ross, Major J. C.
Austin, A. E.	Foster, Lt-Col. W.W.	Lockyer, H.F.	Rounsefell, F. W.
Anderson, Ashworth	Galer, H.N.	London, T.W.B.	St. John, C.W.
Baker, F.	Gehrke, J.W.	Millar, R.M.	Senkler, J.H.
Bell-Irving, Col. H.	Gibson, George F.	Mather, J.D.	Shellshear, Thos.
Bengough, Percy	Glenwright, G.J.	McAllister, Angus	Shortt, J.W.
Boultbee, W. W.	Gordon, Merton C.	Macdonald, Dr. J.A.	Showler, Bert
Brettel, Eric	Griffith, Julius	McDonald, Gen. H.F.	Spencer, Victor
Budd, H. R.	Hall, J.Z.	McGregor, Fred	Taylor, Herbert
Burnett, Dr. W. B.	Harvey, J.N.	McIntosh, Maj. G.H.	Thorn, Major J.C.
Burns, W. E.	Harvey, Hamilton	McIntosh, Dr. J.W.	Tupper, Sir Charles H.
Cameron, H. Murray	Henderson, Henry I.	McNair, D.Y.	Tupper, Reginald
Carmichael, W. R.	Henderson, Stanley	McNeill, A.H., K.C.	Tweedale, Capt. Cyril
Chaffey, George E.	Hodgson, R.C.	McPhillips, L.G.	Twiss, W.J.
Coburn, Arthur	Hutchinson, James	McRae, J.J.	Watson, John
Conway, Capt. W. J.	James, Edwin A.	Nelson, John	Watts, W.
Coote,Col. Leslie	James, Ernest Walter	Nixon, James	Weldon, John
Crip, Frederick	James, Victor C.	Olson, Oscar	Whiteside, A.
Cull, Norman G.	Jameson, E.C.	Plommer, J.J.	Wittall, Norman
Davis, Ghent	Keate, W.L.	Partington, H.R.	Winch, Charles V.
Davis, E. P., K.C.	Kent, Daryl H	Parkins, George C.	Wickens, Charles W.
DeLong, A. Z.	Lawson, W. A.	Roaf, John H.	Woodward, W.C.
			Young, J. Haydn

rang true and the charges did not. The committee included many prominent Vancouver citizens of the era, all male. Their names were well-known and remain evident today in street names and buildings around the city: J.L.G. Abbott, Colonel H. Bell-Irving, Colonel Victor Spencer, W.H. Tupper, W.C. Woodward, Harry Senkler, W.W. Boultbee, Dr. J.W. McIntosh, E.P. Davis KC, and Dr. J.A. Macdonald. The list represented the top people in law, business, industry, medicine, finance, real estate, and other sectors of B.C. life. They had been Conservatives and Liberals before the Provincial Party was born, and their mass defection was unheralded in provincial politics.

The birth of the new party was ominous for Premier Oliver and opposition leader Bowser. In the following months they watched, worried, and targeted McRae as the main opponent rather than each other. The PP had made a very auspicious entry onto the stage, and it certainly wasn't short of money for mounting a major campaign. The next election, expected in a year, loomed as a history maker. Were the old-line political ties about to be broken in B.C.?

A bombshell was dropped at the Provincial Party's first full convention in Vancouver on December 4, 5, and 6, 1923 when it was stated that McRae had decided to retire as the party leader. A shocked hush fell over the hall. Many shouted "No, no!" as delegates wondered what was wrong. McRae stepped up and made his case. He told the members that since the PP was formed he had provided $39,897.23 of the $47,548.25 that had been spent to date. McRae had lots of money and he wasn't complaining about the cost, but he felt this impression of a one-man band could work against him and the PP in the next election. He said his opponents could brandish this fact when he took office, saying that he had bought the premiership and, he added confidently, that victory was going to be theirs. McRae said another fact the old-line parties would hammer on was that he had more money tied up in lumber than anybody else in the province.

McRae also argued that despite growing support, there still was not the support the PP should expect from some quarters, namely people with money to donate so as to ensure that party funding came not from just one man. While wanting to step down as leader, McRae said he would be happy to be a candidate at the next election. Delegates enthusiastically wanted him as leader of the PP, so there was much scurrying about and backroom discussions to find a way around this unexpected development. Finally, a party leading light came up happily with the answer: It was proposed that McRae become president of the Provincial Party Association with the question of leader to be decided by the vote of the party's successful candidates at the upcoming election. It was asserted there was nothing more democratic than this plan. There was a roar of applause and McRae became president.

McRae's money message was also heard loud and clear. Within minutes of being asked, delegates had pledged another $33,225 to the party, a sufficient amount to cover expenses for the next year. The president also stated that he would "use his efforts" to ensure that PP funding was adequate.

Delegates were happy with party progress. They were told there were 22,500 members at convention time, and that membership from outside Vancouver was growing at a rate of 500 a week. Much of this was because the bulk of the money already spent, some $7,000, had gone into "advertising and direct propaganda." The party members had organized 300 meetings across the province. Circulation of the *Searchlight* had gone from 10,000 copies for the first edition to 30,000 for the sixth. They had mailed out some 90,000 copies of the party manifesto and platform.

The resolutions passed at the convention reflected much of what McRae had stated at the New Westminster meeting earlier in the year, which the Committee of 100 had unanimously backed. On Oriental immigration, these responsible and influential men held to the same view as the majority of British Columbians—from bankers, lawyers, and teachers to clergy, blue-collar workers, and union bosses. They wanted them out of the province, and Canada free from the growing spectre of the "yellow peril." While differing in what approach to take, the delegates "were unanimous in their determination to pledge the

Provincial Party to take steps to rid the province once and for all of the Oriental menace to its happiness and prosperity." The Chinese were held largely responsible by many people for the spreading use of narcotics, which unquestionably lay behind the convention resolving that all drug peddlers be subjected to the lash along with severe prison terms.

Delegates also approved a resolution calling on the government to order a royal commission into the charges raised about PGE financing. Premier Oliver finally agreed, but a combination of restrictions imposed on the commissioner, plus the loss of books and other documents that somehow were destroyed in "fires" or in weather related mishaps, resulted—to no one's great surprise—in the commissioner's conclusion that the company was as clean as a train whistle. A large body of people remained convinced, however, that it was a monstrous boondoggle. The PGE continued to be derided as the "Please Go Easy" and "Prince George Eventually." The big loser was McRae, in the amount of $40,000, in 1926 when he lost a libel suit launched by one of the politicians he had cited. He felt, however, that it was money well spent to bring the railway saga and its murky dealings to the attention of everyone in B.C.

A combination of powerful support by former Liberals and Tories, smooth organization and public relations know-how, more than adequate funding, and a growing number of the people seemingly turning to the PP in the hopes of something new and different, gave Oliver and Bowser lots to worry about as they faced 1924, an election year.

1924—Politics Turns Nasty

McRae's money was in play as people were hired to spread the Provincial Party word throughout the province and to recruit the right candidates for the upcoming election. Newspapers saw the PP initially as a curiosity, although their views began to change as the party picked up strength. In the end, however, they didn't drop their support of the old-line parties. On May 10, 1924, when Oliver called voting day for June 20, McRae's movement had a respectable list of candidates for all the ridings. The House standings for the 47 ridings at dissolution were: Liberals 25, Conservatives 14, Independents 4, Socialists 3, and one vacant. The curtain rose on a donnybrook as 167 candidates, including a record seven women, battled it out.

It was a campaign without a charismatic personality at the top. Many Liberals and Tories wished they had gone into the campaign with new, more inspired leaders, but they were stuck with what they had. McRae was new with some fresh ideas, but he was not a charismatic figure, and his money-making past trailed him. Oliver recognized the new McRae challenge and spewed much of his venom on the PP leader rather than on old, tired Bowser. On May 15 the *Vancouver Sun* reported that the premier told a meeting, "General McRae is absolutely unworthy of the slightest credence or support from the people of B.C. He has initiated and at enormous cost is maintaining a malicious campaign and the motive is not far to seek. I ask you if it is your judgment that such a man as he should be allowed to repeat the exploitation of people such as he practiced in

Port Mann and other places." He also asked if McRae actually was shilling for some large corporation, a preposterous suggestion, but still one that union and socialist voters were more than ready to believe.

The extent of anti-Asian feeling in the province emerged as an issue; the number of such people employed at McRae's enterprises was constantly questioned. McRae was no different from Premier Oliver and all the other candidates who felt threatened by the "yellow peril." Oliver maintained that at McRae's Golden mill in the Interior 35 percent of the work force was Chinese rather than the 8 percent McRae claimed—a figure he stuck to in arguing with the premier. The *Victoria Colonist* reported that in an attack on federal immigration policy, McRae told an audience that if he had his way he would put a load of Chinese on a train for Toronto and another load on a train for Montreal "so that people there would have it brought home to them how unpleasant the question could be." Alternatively, he said that every Chinese arriving in B.C. could be given a train ticket to Eastern Canada.

The *Victoria Colonist* also reported that McRae attracted a standing-room-only crowd to the Royal Victoria Theatre where he held the stage for an hour and a half. It was an era for long, long speeches. In a town where old political ties were tight the paper said the reception accorded him "was cordial even to perfection."

The Liberal-supporting *Victoria Times* sniped at McRae's call for lower taxes. It said that between 1920 and 1923 he had never paid more than $206 to the provincial coffers, and nothing at all in 1921. It said people were hoping for lower taxes, but asked, "Surely General McRae, who last year paid the provincial treasury $18.70 and lives in splendour in Vancouver, isn't asking for lower taxes?"

The *Victoria Times* went on to say, "If he ever possessed any qualities as a leader he lost them when he started making millions out of struggling prairie settlers and out of B.C. promotions and Port Mann lots. Who is there in B.C. who has not lost money at Port Mann himself nor has relatives and friends who have not?" Calling for the return of the Liberal government, the paper said a win at the polls by the PP would mean "the leadership of General McRae which on the face of it means a costly experiment."

At the same time, McRae and his candidates were trumpeting throughout the province the claims that the Tories and Liberals had awful records, citing mismanagement and outright criminal activity in the handling of public money. It was a lively contest with some unusual twists. At a meeting starring Premier Oliver at the Pantages Theatre in Victoria, lawyer D.S. Tait stood up and demanded to be allowed to speak on McRae's behalf, something that had seldom, if ever, happened before. In a surprising, open-minded way, Oliver decided to let him speak. After ten minutes and as Tait launched into an assault on the premier and his policies, the organizers decided they had heard enough. But the windy lawyer wouldn't quit. As a Liberal supporter tried to manhandle him off the stage he made a grab for Oliver's papers. The struggling Tait wasn't prepared to go easily; the wrestling match that developed on stage threatened to become the highlight of the night. As the ruckus continued, an astute pianist hit the first notes of "God Save the King." The patriotic tenor of the times demanded that the fisticuffs stop while everyone in the hall stood to attention and bellowed the anthem; then the session closed without further furor as the clock struck midnight. It had been a long evening that began at 8 p.m.

In an enthusiastic moment McRae claimed the party had sixteen sure seats in Vancouver and Victoria, although he didn't make a prediction for the rest of the province. "On election night we are going to drive the grafters out," he maintained. There were, however, many unknown factors in this election, chief among them being the way people would actually vote at the ballot boxes despite what their stated intentions might have been. This new party was vastly different than anything before it and totally untried. Public opinion seemed to be with them, however, and the PP had attracted some strong candidates to the cause. McRae was running for one of six Vancouver seats along with some fourteen others; the top half-dozen garnering the most votes would be the winners.

Sensing the winds of change, bigger than usual crowds jammed Vancouver's downtown streets in front of the *Sun* and the *Province* offices on June 20 to watch as the latest returns from the polling booths were posted. There were changes, but the results were a disaster for McRae and the PP. Their candidates were slaughtered with only four of the 48 being elected; although they had garnered almost 25 percent of the popular vote and acted as a spoiler, splitting the outcome in several ridings. McRae was one of the winning four in Vancouver along with A. McCreery, and two PP candidates were elected in the Interior. McRae was the only leader to be recorded a winner that night, as both Oliver and Bowser went down to defeat. The Liberals didn't have a majority, but could hang onto power with support from independent members. True-blue Conservatives turned livid as they upped their denunciation of "turn-coat McRae," who they claimed cost them the power of office.

McRae was a fairly narrow winner, the last of the six elected to represent the Vancouver area. Among the losers was Oliver's woman cabinet member, Mary Ellen Smith. The *Province,* presciently or suspiciously, said to watch for the upcoming count of the out-of-town, absentee ballots from those who voted prior to June 20. Not too many upsets were expected because absentees usually voted in about the same percentages as did the popular vote on election day.

The fact that the strength of the next government was still unclear didn't seem to matter in true-blue Victoria, bastion of the Empire. The day after the election, political events were shuffled off the front page in the *Victoria Times* in favour of a story about the Royal Navy, which was on a Pacific coast goodwill trip. The battleships *Hood* and *Repulse* and the Australian cruiser HMAS *Adelaide* sailed into the capital with much cheering and fanfare. The *Times'* opening paragraph of the headline story, complete with pictures, warmed the cockles of British Columbian hearts. It read, "The British Special Services Squadron on its passage up the Straits of Juan de Fuca presented this morning the finest example and living symbol, of the power of the Mother Country." Oliver had gone down with his political guns blazing, but it really didn't seem to matter all that much; Britannia still ruled where it counted.

The *Province* said the PP's campaign strategy of household mailings and billboards seemed to have been highly effective. They hadn't won all that many seats, but after coming from nowhere, they had won a significant percentage of the popular vote. The strategy was derived in part from what McRae had learned during his 1918 British Ministry of Information assignment. The paper didn't seem miffed that the strategy involved very little newspaper advertising.

McRae and his supporters began to wonder what was going on as July approached and the absentee ballots still hadn't been counted. No explanation was forthcoming from election officials. A *Province* editorial said ominously that the long, undue delay presented an "opportunity for manipulation." Many were asking questions, but no clear answer ever came from the returning officer.

On July 18 the fears of the new PP were realized. The ballots showed that in Vancouver Mary Ellen Smith had reached a total of 9,251 votes, which meant that McRae was out with only 9,071, trailing fellow PP member Creery who was sixth. McRae denounced the result, saying it was outrageous that the Liberals had appeared to carry so much of the absentee ballot. His disappointment voiced, he soon became more restrained, saying he really wasn't surprised at the outcome because the government had obviously been preparing for this final result ever since election night. In other words, they knew ballot-box manipulation would win. Surprisingly, McRae accepted what had happened as the politics of the time. He didn't ask for a recount or demand a judicial inquiry, and the sound and fury from others died away quickly. Further protest seemed futile.

Had McRae entered the Legislature with three other members, the face of B.C. politics would have been changed dramatically. The percentage of the popular vote the party had received was strong and would have been something to build on. McRae would have had the prestige of leadership and the platform of the Legislature to advance his policies and attack his opponents. The absentee vote, however, was the death knell of the PP and its one and only appearance on the B.C. scene. Whether McRae quickly tired of provincial politics or whether the Advisory Committee of 100 broke up, deciding one shot was enough, was never quite clear. The strong showing in overall votes couldn't overcome the defeat of the founder and driving force of the PP or the loss of all other candidates except three.

The final results left the Conservatives with seventeen seats, a gain of three from the previous House, but not good enough to win over the Liberals' 23. The other seats were taken by three representatives from the PP, three Labour, one Independent, and one Independent Liberal. Bowser was through. A Liberal backbencher in the Interior quickly took a dive to create a by-election and a possible seat for Oliver, who still had his party's support if not their enthusiasm.

Ever the pragmatist, McRae's political aspirations had not completely died. He quietly started a kiss-and-make-up approach to the Conservatives, the more practical of whom were ready to forgive and forget. McRae's comeback began by helping finance a Tory candidate in the by-election held to give Oliver a seat. Oliver won, but McRae had put up his money—his olive branch—and he was back in the party's good graces.

A Murder in Blanche's House

For various reasons, McRae was anxious to keep a low profile following his defeat in the provincial election. He had suffered enough public scrutiny and political backbiting to last him quite a while. So far he had managed to keep his family away from any hint of scandal or misconduct, but it had required some careful manoeuvring. Blanche's marriage to a Roman Catholic had been done quietly, out of town. The three girls had been sent off to Bryn Mawr, the same school their mother had attended, and each returned to Vancouver to join the ranks of young wealthy women who frequented the Jericho Country Club on Saturdays and were invited to dances each weekend in the stately homes of Shaughnessy. They were a part of the flapper generation: spoiled, headstrong, and out to have fun. This was especially true in the years before they were married, and there is no doubt that McRae had a few anxious moments.

Fanta Tait (later Verchere), born in Vancouver in 1906, remembers the years after the First World War.

> Father took us to Britain in 1914 and we spent the war years there, coming back to Vancouver after it was all over. I was a teenager then and bursting to share the social life that swirled around us. There were parties all the time and people flocked to the Jericho Country Club or the Shaughnessy Golf and Country Club which were the best places in town to be seen. In fact, you had to reserve a Saturday night table a

month in advance at Jericho. The Vancouver Hotel was the top spot for large formal functions and it's a shame they tore the first one down at Granville and Georgia. It was much grander than the one we have now. There were coming-out and graduation parties, birthday balls and anniversaries, weddings and christenings, any excuse was good enough for a celebration. The parties at the big houses were like a competition, each hostess vying to give the best party of the season, serving the finest wines, the fanciest food and providing the latest music. Most women owned five or six evening dresses, you needed that many or you would be wearing the same thing all the time.

Everyone knew the McRae girls, Blanche, Lucile, and Peggy. Their father had been called a 'merchant prince' and they certainly were like princesses. They had more to spend than anyone else and were often referred to as 'fast girls.' That phrase didn't mean what it does today, I suppose now you'd call them swingers. They wore extravagant, expensive clothes, smoked, drank, and were driven around town by a chauffeur. There were loads of servants at Hycroft. It was always a delight to be invited to a party in the ballroom, and when you got to know General McRae he was a warm, friendly man and a wonderful host.

Vancouver was much smaller then and we knew each other better. We were quite a group but there aren't many left now, just a few like Naomi Hopkins, Janet McBeath and Eleanor Malkin maybe.

McRae had expected his second daughter Lucile to have a traditional wedding, and her mother wanted a big reception at Hycroft; but instead, as McRae toured the province campaigning for the Provincial Party, she had eloped with her American fiancé, Dwight Paul, who was from Renton, Washington. They were married there on May 31, 1924. Unwilling to wait for the election to be settled as her father had requested, and in true flapper fashion, she had gone ahead and taken care of the matter herself. No mention was made of the wedding in Vancouver's newspapers; however, a luncheon where Lucile was the guest of honour was held at the Jericho Country Club, hosted by Lila Malkin. There is no doubt that her friends Marg Stewart, Allison King, Cora Wootten, Catherine Fordham, and Mrs. Sally Nichol all knew the reason for the luncheon. Lucile's older sister Blanche Baker was on holiday in Europe with her husband at the time, but Blanche's sisters-in-law Doreen Baker and Nano Baker both attended the luncheon. The names of these guests were all that ever appeared in the newspapers; no mention was made of Lucile's marriage, although there was much talk in the neighbourhood about what might have been the reason for the elopement. Ever anxious to keep the family happy, it was not long before McRae had the young couple to the house along with Dwight's mother, who was from Rochester, New York.

By this time McRae's first granddaughter, Jocelyn Baker, had been born, and it was not long before Blanche Beverly Paul, known throughout her life as "Bebe" Paul, was also born. McRae had had three daughters, and he also had three granddaughters: the third was Jocelyn's sister, Audrey Baker, born in 1926.

With the failed provincial election behind him and his daughter's sudden disappearance resolved, McRae gave a sigh of relief, sat back, and tried to relax for a while, but it was not to be. In the late summer of 1924 events conspired against him to bring the family once more into the spotlight. It did not shine directly on them, but it was too close for comfort. Most involved were Blanche and Richard Baker's houseboy, Wong Foon Sing, and Blanche's brother and sister-in-law, Fred and Doreen Baker.

About a month after the Provincial Party was shattered in the election, and as Blanche suggested to a friend, "Dad was fiddled out of his win," a murder occurred in the house at 3851 Osler Avenue and Wong Foon Sing became the principal suspect. Fred Baker with his wife Doreen and their young baby Rosemary had agreed to occupy their house while Richard and Blanche were away in Europe. They had been in residence since May and the houseboy Wong continued to live in his basement room, keeping the house clean and providing meals, which were his normal duties. It had been Richard's idea to hire Wong. He came highly recommended, was very capable, courteous, and an excellent cook, but he came into a lot of grief when the younger Bakers moved in. Baby Rosemary's nurse, Janet Smith, a Scots nursemaid, was the one found dead in the basement laundry room, shot through the head supposedly with a gun owned by Fred Baker, although nobody ever proved that point.

Wong Foon Sing found the nursemaid's body a few minutes before noon on Saturday, July 26, 1924; it was front page news in all the newspapers by Monday morning. Only a day later, *The Evening Star* managing editor Victor Odlum, who was also a Liberal opponent of Alexander McRae and a general from World War One, made the connection from the Baker family to the McRaes. Soon the family history of all the McRaes became fodder for reporters.

Fred, Doreen, and baby Rosemary moved back to the old Baker home in the West End on Monday, July 28 as had been previously planned because Richard and Blanche Baker were returning by train the same morning. The vacationers returned to find their home in a state of chaos. It was the day scheduled for the inquest into the death of Janet Smith. McRae insisted his daughter and son-in-law stay at Hycroft for a few days, but that didn't prevent Blanche from having to appear at the inquest the day she returned. The whole family heaved a sigh of relief when the coroner's jury came down with a verdict of accidental death.

That might have been the end of the affair except for the angry Scots community, which couldn't accept a gunshot wound as accidental, and for *The Evening Star's* Victor Odlum who saw a beautiful chance to heap abuse on his old enemy McRae.

During the inquest Blanche had explained, "We had asked Fred and Doreen to look after our house while we were away. They were newly returned to Vancouver and had been living with Richard's mother. It gave them a chance to be on their own for a while. The house on Osler Avenue is not one of Shaughnessy's grand mansions but quite nice nonetheless. It

The home of Blanche and Richard Baker at 3851 Osler Avenue became one of the most famous addresses in Shaughnessy during 1924 and 1925. While they were vacationing in Europe, Richard's brother Fred lived there with his family and their nanny, Janet Smith, who was found murdered in the basement. The ensuing charges, arrests, trials, libel suits, and counter suits made newspaper headlines for nearly a year and a half. The case remains one of Vancouver's most notorious unsolved murders.

has a big porch out front and a wonderfully cozy living room with a big fireplace and beamed ceiling. It's near the corner of Osler and Twenty-Fifth, built in the Craftsman style with shingles, dormer windows, and tall chimneys, definitely not the kind of neighbourhood where you would expect to have a murder."

When Fred and Doreen moved in, having recently returned from Great Britain and France where Fred managed an import-export business, he had brought with him his old air force revolver. It was initially kept in a haversack in the front hall and later moved to the attic. That was one of the keys to the whole case, and for months the names of all the Bakers, and often Alexander McRae as well, were bandied about in the newspapers in the midst of what became the scandal of the decade. Newspapers continued to follow the story that seemed to have no end for eighteen months.

Evidence at the inquest revealed that two day's prior to the Bakers' return from the continent, on Saturday morning, July 26, the 22-year-old nursemaid was found dead in the basement laundry room, shot through the head. It happened just before lunch when the houseboy Wong Foon Sing was busy in the kitchen, peeling potatoes for the mid-day meal. He heard the shot and rushed downstairs to find Janet Smith dead. She was lying on her back beside the ironing board where she had been pressing the baby's things. His hands became covered with blood when he tried to raise her head to see if he could help her. Then he dashed back upstairs to phone Fred Baker at his office. Fred immediately called the police, and Wong—not surprisingly—told the doctor and police who arrived on the scene that he was horrified and frightened at what he had found.

Within days a story was making the rounds of Shaughnessy about a Friday night orgy at 3851 Osler where Smith was shot, although there were many facts that made this suggestion highly improbable. The doctor who arrived at the scene about the same time as the police said Janet Smith had been dead no more than an hour. It should have dispelled the rumours, but it was too tempting for General Odlum and his newspaper. It was a chance to increase circulation at the expense of his old military rival General McRae.

Smith was a nursemaid that Fred Baker and his wife had hired while they lived in Britain. Her diaries, which were read during various court enquiries, showed she had more romances than Theda Bara, although some of her escapades may have been more imaginary than real. She had been born in Scotland and worked for Fred and Doreen in Britain. When the couple moved to France for six months in order to close out their business interests there, Janet went with them, and when they returned home to Vancouver she had agreed to come with them again, providing they promised to pay her way back after a year if she didn't like it.

Fred had been in the pharmaceutical and drug business in Europe and had made a hasty retreat when questions started being asked about the legality of some of his business dealings on the continent and in Asia. He maintained he did nothing unlawful; however, the question came up numerous times during the inquest and the court cases after the murder that dragged on for more than a year.

Point Grey police initially suggested that Janet Smith committed suicide (although there were many reasons why this was almost impossible), and the inquest jury decided her death was accidental. The suggestion that Janet Smith committed suicide was likely what incited the Scots community into action; as one voice they insisted she must have been murdered. They represented a large proportion of the Vancouver population at the time, and their voice was strong. Smith's body was exhumed from Mountain View cemetery for a second inquest because of the uproar they caused.

The second inquest came to the conclusion that Janet Smith had been murdered. This second decision immediately turned suspicion on Wong Foon Sing because he was the only one known to have been in the house at the time, and the Scots community loudly proclaimed he must be the murderer and should be charged. About this time the house on Osler Avenue became a curiosity and a long string of curious onlookers began to file down the street at all hours of the day and night. Richard and Blanche had returned to live in the house, but they found the constant attention unnerving.

McRae had been concerned for the welfare of his daughter Blanche and very young granddaughter Jocelyn since their return home. He had insisted the blood be cleaned from the basement floor before they moved back into their house and he had personally checked out the house before their return. Now he decided they would both be safer elsewhere and sent them off on an extended visit to Mama Howe in Minneapolis.

Richard and his brother Fred were pilots during World War One and both of them were shot down. They were daredevils and war heroes of a sort, who had adapted well to the risky business of life in the Royal Flying Corps. In any case, Fred "Leffy" Baker had brought a gun home from the war and took it with him when the family moved temporarily to Osler Avenue.

Fred Baker's version of the crime was a little hard to believe. He suggested that Smith had taken the revolver, which by this time had been stored away in an upstairs cupboard, down to the basement to look at. It hardly seems plausible that curiosity would strike when she was in the middle of the ironing, but Fred seemed to think it could.

The whole affair was complicated by an inept police force that couldn't have caught Jack The Ripper if he had walked up to them with a bloody knife in his hands. They missed seeing a bullet lying on the basement floor, although it was never actually proven that it had been the one that killed Janet Smith. They discovered that Fred's gun, found lying beside the body, was jammed, so it is difficult to see how it could actually have been the murder weapon. It was just assumed to be it. To experiment with the range and velocity of the shooting the police used the skull of an unknown man from the local mental hospital. At headquarters they fired bullets through it to try to match the hole in Smith's head. They used some of the most grisly methods ever recounted by the newspapers, which printed it all, word for word, when the details were revealed in court. The papers said people in attendance at the court turned green when they heard about the experiment; ultimately, it proved nothing.

The Scots played up the idea that Smith was an underpaid, overworked, poor little immigrant girl far from home, being exploited by the Bakers. Fred and Doreen gave her $20 a month, good food, a nice room, and quite a bit of time off. It was more than the average nanny received.

Harry Senkler, one of Vancouver's best lawyers and a friend of McRae, was hired to defend Wong whose uncle had worked for the Senklers for years. The Chinese tong societies put up the money for his defence.

Several of Smith's friends who were employed at other homes in Shaughnessy testified she had told them she was scared of being in the house with Wong, but Senkler said her diaries said nothing about it. Newspapers suggested Janet Smith lived in a fantasy world. She was supposed to be engaged to a local logger, but when he was out of town building what he thought would be their happy honeymoon home, she was often out on the town, dancing with other men. Far from being afraid of Wong, she wrote in her diaries about accepting gifts from him, and it is likely he had a crush on her, although he had a wife and daughter back in China.

The Scots demanded Wong's head, convinced that this evil Chinese man had lusted after a white girl and then murdered her even though there was absolutely nothing in the autopsy to suggest she had been "violated" as the newspapers hinted.

Dissatisfied with the lack of progress in the case the Scots and their societies hired more lawyers and insisted that Attorney General Alex Manson do something. He was a Scot himself and well-known for wanting the Chinese out of B.C. The Scots couldn't understand why the police didn't just charge Wong with murder. The problem was they didn't have any evidence.

The clans made a great spectacle at Smith's funeral and later they raised money for a monument at Mountain View cemetery. At the graveside one minister, during the emotional heat of his eulogy, said it was a time of "holy war" between the Orientals and the whites in Vancouver.

After the two inquests things became even more complicated: Wong had his first run-in with the Scots. It was an August night when he was grabbed by some men in Chinatown, thrown into a car, taken to an office, cross-examined, and beaten when he maintained that he hadn't killed Smith and didn't know anything more than he had already told the coroner. It was the early hours of the morning before he was driven back to the Baker house. It was learned later that a private detective agency, working for the provincial police, had snatched him off the street. Until this time the Chinese had watched and waited for events to unfold; now they too wanted justice.

Things got worse a few days later when a well-known Chinese man was gunned down as he was leaving a restaurant in Chinatown, leading many people from the mayor on down to believe the area was totally out of control. There were stories that the man was assassinated because of troubles among the tongs, some suggesting he was too close to the white authorities and was feeding them information about illegal immigration, smuggling, and gambling. The killer was never found.

Wong continued to live at the Baker home, but many still believed he was a murderer, which resulted in a terrible development on the night of March 24, 1925, some eight months after the murder took place.

Blanche had long since returned from Minnesota and she and Richard had gone out for dinner at the Jericho Country Club. Wong was in the house alone. The baby Jocelyn and her nursemaid were at Hycroft for the evening, a common practice of the time as Chinese houseboys and Scottish nursemaids were not left alone in the home for the evening. When the Bakers returned they noticed nothing unusual but they awoke in the morning to a very cold house. Wong was supposed to look after the furnace and Richard went down to see why there was no heat. He found the houseboy's basement bedroom had been broken into and Wong was gone. Police again swarmed over the house.

Wong's disappearance riled the Chinese who said it was obvious he had been kidnapped. Feelings were running so high that some Chinese believed Wong was at the bottom of the harbour. The Ku Klux Klan had recently announced they were establishing a chapter in Vancouver and that added to the speculation.

Then some unusual characters of the time came into the act. One was John Sedgwick Cowper, an eccentric editor of a weekly gossip sheet, and the other was a shop assistant and part-time fortuneteller named Barbara Orford. She claimed that she had had visions of an orgy at the Osler Avenue house the night before Smith's death, featuring some well-known members of the social set as well as the housemaid who was supposedly hit on the head. Cowper was a fan of the occult and took up her case, printing everything in his paper. Afterwards she changed her story to say that she saw it all—not as a vision—but personally because she had actually been at the house. Cowper kept plugging her story even though she was obviously a con artist. He and others continued to believe her despite Attorney General Manson telling reporters the police had investigated and it was all nonsense.

While this was happening Wong was having the six worst weeks of his life. After being grabbed from the basement he was taken blindfolded to a house near Twenty-Fifth Avenue and Dunbar Street where the kidnappers chained him to the floor of a bedroom. He was treated roughly; once his captors, who wore Ku Klux Klan-style white hooded robes, held a mock hanging and pretended to put a rope around his throat.

After six long weeks chained in a bedroom, Wong was found by police, wandering on Marine Drive near Dunbar Street. It soon was learned that the kidnappers were the same private detectives who had snatched him months earlier. This time they had been hired by the Point Grey police to find out what had happened to Janet Smith. The police and the Point Grey Council had passed $1,400 of the council's money to the detectives. They knew all along what was going on, and so did Attorney General Manson. The detectives had proposed that Wong be kidnapped to try to force a confession from him.

Like a comic opera, the end of the kidnapping episode was hard to believe. One of the men, who said the government had promised him immunity, wrote a letter to the attorney general's special sleuth, complaining that he hadn't been paid as much as he had been promised for the kidnapping. He wanted more money or he would tell his story to the newspapers. Manson's men didn't have much option then but to tell the detectives to free Wong. The poor man went from being a prisoner in a bedroom to a jail cell where he was immediately charged with Smith's murder. The Scots were ecstatic and the Chinese, along with many others, were livid because they thought the poor houseboy was the victim of an awful injustice. Harry Senkler was furious, knowing there wasn't a scrap of evidence to tie Wong to Smith's death. The murder charge was a desperate fishing expedition, and many recognized it for what it was. Senkler even got Wong out on bail, something that was unusual in a murder case.

Finally about a dozen people were charged with kidnapping. It was hard to believe who they were: the chief and two Point Grey police, the reeve and two councillors, some Scottish society members, and the newsman Cowper. The politicians were yelling at each other, the Chinese tongs became threatening, and the Scots were beside themselves. It was clear the government wasn't happy to charge government officials with an offence against a Chinaman when they really wanted to find a white girl's killer, but they didn't have much choice. Fred Baker also launched a slander suit against the newspaperman Cowper because of his stories about orgies on Osler Avenue.

Vancouver and the McRae family were still feeling the after effects of the murder during the spring, summer, and fall of 1925. A lot of things were happening at once. Some of the lawyers said it was the greatest perversion of justice ever known. The Scottish community was shamefaced when they found their countrymen among those now charged with kidnapping, but it was the Scottish women who then packed the courts to hear all the testimony from the kidnappers. They hissed and booed whatever they didn't like, which was most of it. Senkler was a favourite target as they saw him as a tong-paid defender of a Chinese murderer. To upset them further, the court threw out the murder charge against Wong because there was no evidence that he had killed the unfortunate girl.

Characteristic of the times, and to no one's surprise, the police, the politicians, and Cowper were found not guilty of kidnapping. The jury's decision infuriated one judge, who told the panel they had no choice but to return a guilty verdict, but they defied him and brought in a not guilty decision. Two members of the kidnap gang from the detective agency were sent to jail for about a year, the newspaperman John Sedgwick Cowper was fined for slander, and that was the end of it.

Wong Foon Sing remained the inscrutable Chinaman until one day he said he was going back to China. His leaving was finally the end of the case.

Peggy McRae Marries

Vancouver's post-war boom had turned to bust for some people by the mid-1920s. It was a strange time, more difficult to explain and understand than the usual cyclical ups-and-downs of the economy. There was unemployment for some and good times for others, creating a wide cleavage in society. In the winter of 1925 there had been 1,800 men on relief in Vancouver, living on 50 cents a day for meals and a bed. While working professionals snapped up 20-foot cruisers for $700, desperate people placed job-wanted ads, offering to work for anything. One woman wanted child-care work, day or night, for 25 cents an hour. Coal was $10 a ton delivered. Stew meat was 17 cents a pound, cod 10 cents, and salmon 15 cents. Room-and-board could be had for $8 a week. A suit at Spencer's Stores was $20 and a four-room bungalow in Kitsilano was for sale for $3,500. Land in Burnaby was $250 an acre. The newspapers featured a sketch of a proposed First Narrows span to cost $3 million. (The Lions Gate Bridge arrived twelve years later.) There were major economic disparities, but by 1926 the economy had started to pick up, trade with the United States was booming, and the "Roaring Twenties" were rolling again.

McRae continued to mull over his future, biding his time before deciding to become involved in politics again, this time on the federal scene. But the McRaes found it difficult to keep their names out of the newspaper headlines. For a change, this time it was a happy story involving the youngest McRae daughter, Peggy. Every young blade and flapper in town gobbled up

All three McRae girls attended private school in the United States. Peggy (left) and Lucile are pictured at their school in White Sulphur Springs, West Virginia, 1921.

the details as the forthcoming McRae wedding was announced. Mary Margaret "Peggy" McRae was to be married February 15, 1926. The spectacle was the highlight of the winter social season. The *Vancouver Province* called the wedding, "Vancouver's most widely discussed romance" while the *Vancouver Sun* described it as the "most artistically beautiful ever to be held in the city." It was certainly celebrated on a grand scale; some said the only thing finer would have been a royal wedding.

McRae's youngest daughter was born in Toronto in January 1906, the only one of his three girls born in Canada. She was also the only one who attended school in Europe as the other two had graduated from Bryn Mawr and then returned home. They were now both married.

This wedding was McRae's and Blaunche's only chance to celebrate the marriage of one of their daughters at home amongst close friends, and they were prepared to make it an occasion to remember. Peggy had been the imp of the family, her exploits in school were legendary, and she was famous for the three huge Great Dane dogs that slept on blankets on the floor of a closet in her room. Like her mother, Peggy was an experienced equestrian and she often travelled with her mother to horse shows in California and Oregon, and later when she was older, in Great Britain and Europe. The young girl had been persuaded that she

129

should attend school in Paris in order to perfect her French. Here she befriended a young woman whose name was Katherine Van Herckelon and the two of them became inseparable. On the way home from school in the spring of 1924, while her father was running for election in B.C. and just as her sister Lucile was eloping, Peggy stopped in New York for a visit with Katherine's family, and this was how she met the girl's uncle Walter Seligman. The girls were accompanied on the voyage across the Atlantic by Peggy's oldest sister Blanche and her husband Richard Baker who were on their way home to Osler Avenue and the events which ensued there, but the arrival of the group in New York marked the beginning of Peggy's whirlwind romance with Katherine's uncle Walter.

Although Peggy was the only McRae daughter born in Canada, she—like her sisters—made frequent visits to see Mama Howe in Minneapolis. One of these visits took place in 1912 when she was six years of age.

Walter Seligman was a descendant of one of New York's oldest families and also one of the three large Jewish banking families in New York at the time. The Seligmans were well-known in both New York and Palm Springs, where Walter's mother resided for part of the year. They also owned a country place at Deal, in New Jersey, a community favoured by many wealthy Jewish families as a summer retreat. The visit of several McRae family members to the Seligman home in New York was met with approval by all concerned.

The couple was described as almost complete opposites. Peggy was seen as outgoing, flamboyant, spoiled, and mischievous; Walter was responsible, reserved, confident, and a product of the best that New York could provide. Blanche reported to her mother that Walter literally swept Peggy off her feet with his sophistication, his influential friends, and his lifestyle in New York, which was much more exciting than small time Vancouver.

The courtship involved extensive visits first in New York and later in Vancouver, where Seligman arrived for an extended visit in the fall of 1925. The Janet Smith affair was no longer making news in the papers and it is possible the date for his visit was selected with some care in order to ensure any mention of the murder was over and done with. In any case, women's page writers took up Peggy's romantic tale with enthusiasm especially when the couple went riding accompanied by Peggy's huge dogs. The McRaes of Hycroft entertained lavishly that fall as they introduced Walter Seligman and Katherine Van Herckelon to Peggy's friends and some of Alexander's business associates and compatriots. Mama Howe arrived from Minneapolis to take part in the festivities. There were swimming parties in the mews, and dances and dinners every evening.

By the time Walter and Katherine were ready to return to New York, the romance had become the talk of the town, and social page writers waited expectantly for the wedding announcement. No one was disappointed, nor was anyone surprised, when Peggy's engagement was announced before the train carrying Walter and Katherine left for the East.

McRae was once more faced with a marriage of mixed religious faiths but this one was a little easier to resolve than the first one had been. He consulted with a close friend, a chaplain from his army days who agreed to perform the ceremony. With some minor adjustments the details of the service were sorted out to the satisfaction of both families, and Major Reverend C. A. Williams conducted the ceremony.

It was without question the biggest and most lavish wedding of that year and many others; it was something that no woman living in Vancouver at the time ever forgot. Writers for the social pages of the newspapers couldn't recall anything as grand and glorious as the wedding of Peggy McRae and Walter Seligman, which took place in mid-February 1926. It befitted the daughter of a merchant prince.

The families developed an invitation and announcement list of 2,000 people—1,000 friends of the groom and 1,000 friends of the bride—from Great Britain, France, New York, Florida, Washington, Minnesota, Ontario, B.C., and from cities all across the United States and Canada. Only 1,000 were actually invited to attend the wedding, the other 1,000 were merely told the marriage was taking place. Of course, because they came from around the world and had other commitments, many sent their regrets to the McRae family. Nonetheless, some 500 did participate in the wedding and attendant festivities that took place at Hycroft in February.

Two weeks prior to the ceremony, the *Province* ran a picture of Peggy and five of her nine attendants. Her sisters Blanche and Lucile were pictured as matrons of honour along with Peggy's close Vancouver friends, Allison King, Cora Wootten, and Lila Malkin. The other attendants lived out-of-town. Katherine Van Herckelon, Walter's niece, was maid of honour and the remaining bridesmaids were Peggy's friends from school: Pauline Seidel from Minneapolis, Leslie Tevis from Portland, and Betty Morrison from Seattle. Beneath the group photograph, the newspaper forecasted, "Society is awaiting with interest the outstanding social event of this and many other seasons in the wedding of Miss Margaret McRae, daughter of Gen. and Mrs. A. D. McRae, and Mr. Walter Seligman of New York."

The whirlwind of prenuptial parties began only days into the New Year with teas and showers predominating; everyone who knew the family wanted to attend as many events as possible. It was a heyday for social reporters, as during the 1920s newspapers regularly ran long lists of the names of guests who attended large parties in the belief that these people would all buy a newspaper in order to see their names in print and thereby increase the paper's circulation.

Two days before the grand event there was a rehearsal at Hycroft that the entire wedding party attended. It was followed by a magnificent dinner and pre-wedding celebration for family members and attendants and everyone partied into the wee-small hours.

Blaunche Latimer McRae was famous for entertaining in a grand style and this wedding was her crowning glory. Ivory velvet carpeting edged in gold was installed on the main staircase, through the reception area, and into the main drawing room where the wedding ceremony took place, so it would be in keeping with the colour scheme she and her daughter had chosen for the event. When the day finally arrived one guest remarked in awe that the house looked "like a picture from a child's book of fairy tales." Everywhere there were white blossoms, and the smell of gardenias filled the air. Fourteen ivory tapers banked the magnificent mantle of the fireplace in the drawing room, and the light flickered from crystal chandeliers in every room as beautiful ladies in silver gowns talked with elegantly dressed men in white tie and tails.

February in Vancouver is often rainy, wet, and gloomy. The three greenhouses at Hycroft produced some of the flowers to decorate the house, but many of the blooms were brought in from California and even from Mexico. Every room was filled with blossoms, ranging from ivory roses and pale white heathers, to narcissus, mimosa, lily-of-the-valley, and huge white Easter lilies, orchids, and baby's breath, which cascaded from baskets and urns.

Both the ceremony and reception were held at Hycroft. About 100 witnessed the nuptials and the remaining 400 guests arrived for a gala reception and evening of dancing and celebration in the ballroom. A symphony orchestra played the wedding march and provided music prior to the service and during dinner, while a dance band picked up the tempo for celebrants who arrived later to toast the bride and groom and to wish them bon voyage when they sailed off for a three-month honeymoon in France, Spain, and Italy.

On the grand day, the orchestra arrived in late afternoon and began playing softly for early arrivals. Upstairs the young ribbon girls waited anxiously for the sounds of the music that would tell them it was time to take their places in the reception hall. These

girls were the young daughters of close family friends: Grace
Cameron, Barbara Huntting, Naomi McMullen, and Trudyean and
Louise Spencer. Cautiously, they walked down the white-carpeted
stairway, each one carrying a bouquet and the ribbons they would
hold to form an aisle for the bride and her attendants. As the
minister took his place in front of the fireplace, the groom, the
best man Mr. J. J. Phillips of Los Angeles, and the ushers ranged
themselves on the right. The ushers included Charles Cadley,
M.L.A. Ian Mackenzie, Dr. H. Letson, and the bride's brother-in-
law Richard Baker who—with his wife Blanche—had been in New
York when Peggy first met Walter. Then the strains of the wedding
march drifted through the house and up the stairs where the bride
and her nine attendants waited. Dressed in shining silver lamé,
each in turn took the long walk down the white velvet staircase
across the hall and into the flower-bedecked drawing room,
followed at last by two tiny flower girls in white organdy carrying
rose leaf baskets: Miss Rosemary Baker who was only four and
Miss Jacqueline Baker who was just two. Neither one was quite
sure what they should do, but they threw petals on the ivory carpet
whenever they remembered. Peggy, on the arm of her father, wore
a dress of ivory satin, embroidered with pearls, crystals, and
clusters of rhinestones. Her court train was caught at the shoulders
and decorated to match her dress while a cloud of tulle enveloped
her gown. Bound close to her head with a coronet of orange
blossoms was a bridal veil of old lace. Her bouquet contained white
heather, lily of the valley, white gardenias, and mauve orchids.

The ceremony was not long but included all the traditional
words, and as the groom kissed the bride the orchestra once
again began to play before the couple's assembled friends and
family greeted them. There was much hugging and kissing. A
magnificent dinner prepared by the staff of Hycroft was served
on the flower-bedecked terrace that was fragrant with daffodils
and hyacinths. There were toasts and thank-yous for everyone,
especially the mother-of-the-bride Blaunche McRae, who wore
a dress of magnificent gold-lamé shot with orange threads—one
of her favourite colour combinations. Peggy and Walter cut the
four-tiered cake, which sat on a bed of orchids and lily-of-the-

valley, before distributing a piece to each guest. All the bridesmaids and ribbon girls took their pieces home to place under their pillows in hopes they would soon find the man of their dreams.

The *Province* reported, "More than 100 guests witnessed the lovely ceremony and several hundred others were in attendance at the reception and dance which followed. A dance orchestra dispensed the music and innumerable daffodils and greenery decorated the ballroom. For travel Mrs. Seligman donned a smart tailleur of brown Kasha. The short coat opened over a brown satin jumper. She wore a close fitting hat on simple lines and a blue fox fur completed her costume. After a three-month trip to Spain and southern Europe, the couple will take up residence in New York." The story ended with the comment, "Guests who accompanied Mr. Seligman to Vancouver, not included in the bridal party were Mr. and Mrs. O'Donohue of New York and Mrs. J.J. Phillips."

Peggy and Walter travelled all over Europe after the wedding on a honeymoon fit for royalty. As in a fairytale, the bride also became pregnant, but unfortunately lost the baby prematurely while they were in Paris. Her convalescence was not long. As she left the hospital, however, she was told she could never have another child. It was a factor that would lead to divorce for the couple twenty years later.

Peggy's wedding was a pleasant diversion for McRae. Never long out of the limelight, however, he had decided to embark on a campaign to win a federal seat in Ottawa. This marked another milestone in his life that was propelled by an insatiable desire to investigate new fields of endeavour, to climb new mountains, and—this time—to contribute to the betterment of his country and his fellow countrymen. He had wanted to improve the lot of British Columbians, but that opportunity had been denied him. Now with some political experience and a disappointing loss behind him, he decided to enter politics at the national level.

McRae, Byng, and Valentino

The flappers cried, moviegoers sighed, and the news was the talk of the town. On August 23, 1926, the "Roaring Twenties" were brought to a hush by the death of a matinee idol. Everyone talked in subdued, reverent tones about Rudolph Valentino. He of the dark, smouldering eyes and god-like good looks. It was hard to believe he was gone, no more to dash across the screen as a passionate sheik, sweeping maidens off across the sands to his boudoir. His fans could only imagine what went on at the oasis after his tent door flap closed but each one had built her own dream sequence around the familiar scenario. Valentino was the biggest name on the silent screen, and his death in New York was totally unexpected. It devastated his star-struck fans. In Canada, a federal election campaign was underway—but who really cared?

Valentino's demise was the headline story in the *Vancouver Sun*, with another front-page item recounting the heady night two years earlier when the biggest male star of the silent flicks made a personal appearance in Vancouver and many normally reserved women threw caution to the wind. Valentino appeared at the Denman Street arena. In keeping with his movie image, his dressing room was a tent erected outside the building. The *Sun* told its readers that "2,000 women stormed the dressing room tent and tore the canvas to ribbons in their effort to get a glimpse of the famous sheik." Like a thunderous movie melodrama the scene grew tense. It took the best efforts of police and firemen to get Valentino from the shredded tent into the

136

safety of the manager's office. The star, whose sexy tango had aroused a generation of young women, was accompanied by his third wife and dancing partner who had the most unglamorous and un-Latin name of Winifred Hudnut. Despite the chaos, and the threat to life and limb, Valentino presented a beauty contest prize to the ecstatic Patsy Henderson and a dancing prize to nimble-footed Mr. and Mrs. Vaughan Moore.

McRae, who at one time wore an Arab costume at one of his lavish New Year's Eve fancy-dress balls, was no match for Valentino. The only mention of his campaign was a small story on an inside page, reporting that McRae spoke to a Women's Conservative Club meeting in North Vancouver at the home of Mrs. W.L. Keane. Following his nomination as the Tory candidate, he said, "I would rather that a local man had been honoured with the nomination. You have selected me, however, and I can assure you that I will leave no stone unturned in my campaign to contest the riding." Despite the bitter taste of his first and questionable provincial political defeat, McRae was eager to plunge back in and had worked quietly since 1924 to get into the Conservative Party's good books to obtain a nomination. As always, his ready donations to party coffers helped. The riding of North Vancouver had been created through national electoral redistribution in 1924. It embraced all of North and West Vancouver and the Sunshine Coast as far as Powell River. A Liberal, who had moved in order to contest a Vancouver city riding, had won it in the last election.

McRae was accompanied to the North Vancouver meeting by Leon Ladner, one of the area's leading respected Conservatives who gave much needed assurances to the audience that the general was back in the fold. There were some who never forgave him for deserting the Conservative Party in order to form his own late unlamented Provincial Party. The pragmatists knew however that McRae had shown some appeal in his first attempt at elected office and, of course, there was all his money that would bankroll a strong personal campaign in the federal battle.

The *Province* reported a marathon two-hour speech that McRae gave in a jam-packed Lonsdale Theatre in North Vancouver on August 24. McRae slammed the Ottawa Liberals for not taking steps to bring fairness to the system of freight rates and promised that a new Conservative government would take immediate action. The general stated he had widely criticized the Pacific Great Eastern Railway (PGE) but was not in favour of scrapping it. He said that over the years B.C. had paid its share of federal taxes for road building in eastern Canada, and he felt the rail line should receive a $6 million subsidy from Ottawa. He was soundly applauded when he took up one of his favourite topics: development of the Peace River country. McRae stressed that immigration efforts should be spent on British and other European citizens, and that they should be brought to B.C. via the Panama Canal rather than by a long cross-country train ride.

He was among the first to call for development of the Garibaldi area as a park, but that it "should be a great national park not a provincial affair." He declared that creating a park of the stature this alpine area required would be an expensive endeavour, but would become a great asset for Canada and B.C. He hailed the tourist potential of the area and maintained that travellers should be encouraged to explore it through advertising by the federal government's foreign offices. McRae was possibly the first to suggest that a new Tory government would consider building a road from North Vancouver, as an extension of the Grouse Mountain Road, stretching between the Howe Sound and Fraser Valley watersheds all the way to the base of Mount Garibaldi and thence up to Lake Garibaldi. He also proposed a road that would connect Squamish and Vancouver.

His vision was once again far ahead of public demand, encompassing the future long before it became a reality. It was to be another half-century before development reached this area and the now internationally famous Whistler-Blackcomb ski resort was begun. The Vancouver-Squamish route suggested by McRae has been talked about for many years, particularly since Whistler-Blackcomb has become the highest rated skiing community in North America. The existing coastal road up Howe Sound gets busier each year and results in some 400 motor vehicle accidents annually.

While McRae campaigned in the west, Canada was in a state of political turmoil at the federal level. There had arisen the famous King-Byng battle when Governor General Lord Byng exercised what he believed was his constitutional power and refused to grant the dissolution of Parliament sought by Prime Minister Mackenzie King, who wanted a new election. Instead, Byng gave Opposition Leader Arthur Meighan the opportunity to form a Conservative government. Within three days Meighan had lost in Parliament, setting up a fall election, which was won by King. His term was the shortest of any Canadian prime minister. Meighan governed from June 28 only until September 25, 1926. Although he had previously been prime minister for eighteen months in 1920 and 1921. Lord Byng's decision had infuriated King, who hammered away at it during the campaign. It also triggered an unending debate among constitutional experts as to whether the governor-general exceeded his authority as the Liberal leader claimed.

McRae moved to North Vancouver for the duration of the campaign to conduct the fierce battle that ensued when popular Gerry McGeer was nominated by the Liberals to run for the same seat. He was the same man who three years earlier had written a slashing, abusive assessment of McRae in a letter to Premier Oliver.

Despite McRae's money and his hired campaign workers who were already tramping the riding, the Liberals thought he was beatable because some Conservatives might not forgive him for deserting them and might in annoyance decline to vote. McRae predicted a Tory landslide, while the *Sun* believed that most people "would salute the general but vote for McGeer."

Still smarting from his run-in with McRae and the PP, Premier Oliver added his voice to the federal fray repeating the charges he had raised in the 1924 provincial tussle—criticizing McRae's money, his business practices, and his Tory turncoat past.

On August 26 the papers said the Liberals attracted the biggest political rally in Powell River so far; this was an area the party felt was pivotal in the election. They were wary of the left-wing attraction of a Labour Party candidate in this town of unionized workers. Oliver quoted from a letter sent by McRae to Attorney General Manson (who had rejected the opportunity to debate with McRae in 1923), in which the general stated that any person presenting himself for public office should be able to show himself worthy of public confidence. The premier said McRae didn't fit the bill.

Oliver also quoted from editions of the now defunct *Searchlight*, which he said contained hundreds of pages of the violent slander published by McRae and his associates, abusing both the Liberals and Tories, and yet "today you have him here as the candidate of one of the parties he abused and vilified three years ago." Oliver said that many people overseas lost $2 million in bonds when the Canadian North Pacific Fisheries went under. He also maintained there were many at home who paid $5,000 for Port Mann lots that were eventually given up for $50 in owed taxes. "All these people lost money while McRae boasted that he spent $25,000 a year to live in palatial splendour at Hycroft," he said. It was a bitter and vindictive campaign where Oliver constantly harped on the Port Mann issue.

McGeer attacked McRae's military career with snide comments and jokes at a Powell River meeting that even some of his own people criticized. He tried to skirt around the issue by claiming, "I have never referred to it in a serious vein in any address." Of course not; he got all his digs through laughter and ridicule. Even McRae's old political foe, Victor Odlum, writing in the *Vancouver Star*, was critical of the jokes; he drew petulant complaints from McGeer about being attacked by his own side.

On voting day there were four candidates in the race: McRae, McGeer, Labour candidate W.C. Lefeux, and an obscure last minute entry, James Gill. Again there were thousands in the streets outside the *Sun* and the *Province* downtown offices to watch the results as they were posted. Vancouver North went as many expected. Lefeux attracted enough of the left-wing with 1,363 votes to ensure McRae could beat McGeer by 692 votes— 5,080 to 4,388. Unlike most of the country, B.C. went Conservative, winning twelve of the fourteen west coast seats, while across Canada the voters returned the Mackenzie King

Liberals. It was the same story on the prairies where the three provinces remained solidly Liberal and returned only one Conservative in Alberta. Tory leader Arthur Meighan went down to personal defeat and was through. The final House standings were: Liberals, 116; Conservatives, 91; Progressives, 13; United Farmers of Alberta, 11; Liberal Progressives, 9; Labour, 3; and Independents, 2.

Savouring his first win at the polls, McRae told the *Province*: "I consider the business of this country of first importance and in my humble opinion the criticism by the Conservative opposition should be first of all constructive. I believe we should facilitate such sound policies as are essential to the prosperity of Canada. While I will be a novice at Ottawa I am going in good company." Liberal warhorse lawyer J.W. de B. Farris didn't agree. He commiserated in the press with the "benighted people of Vancouver" for failing to support the Liberal Party.

A week after the election the *Vancouver Sun* had an article touting McRae as a possible leader to replace Meighan. The paper said he had made a strong showing and "what he lacks in parliamentary debating strength he more than makes up by foresight." It contended that McRae "would command the support of all sections of business life in Canada and his election for this position would have the tonic effect of breathing new life and hope into the Conservative Party."

Late in September McRae had to pay the price for some sweeping allegations he had made in the now defunct *Searchlight*. William Sloan, the provincial minister of mines, was awarded $40,000 in a libel action against McRae for claims of financial wrongdoing made and then printed during the 1924 provincial campaign. It was the largest libel award made by a B.C. jury up to that time.

When the Tory caucus met in Ottawa on October 11 they selected veteran member Hugh Guthrie as the interim leader, pending a full leadership convention, likely to be held in early 1927.

Pick a Winner

As McRae took his seat in Ottawa, *Vancouver Province* reporter Robert Reade filed a story about the man from Hycroft that stated, "Our new rookie MP from the north shore saw a friendly face the first time he sat down in Parliament, but it was on the other side of the floor." The Liberal government's John Campbell Elliott and McRae had been schoolmates in Glencoe almost a half century earlier. Elliott was a lawyer before moving into Ontario provincial politics and then to the federal scene as a minister in Mackenzie King's cabinet.

McRae quietly assumed his seat in Parliament, looking forward to a new adventure in a new milieu. He watched carefully, enjoying the pageantry of the proceedings, learning the rules of protocol, fascinated by the posturing and interplay that seemed to play such a large role in his new position. He soon appreciated that he was now involved in an entirely different game. Party bigwigs were well aware of McRae's record and reputation as an organizer and strategist and as a man who didn't hesitate to go after what he wanted with cool, confident determination, and they desperately needed someone to get their leaderless group back on track. Hugh Guthrie was holding the reins temporarily, but he wasn't the man for the long haul. Party leaders knew that McRae had bolted to form his own Provincial Party, so there were some who looked on him with misgivings. But there was a tough job to do and political pragmatism dictated that McRae could play a key role in the Conservative's future.

He moved up quickly in the party; on April 13 he was named chairman of the executive committee for the upcoming national convention. This was too fast for some old-line Tories who felt he hadn't served an adequate apprenticeship and needed more indoctrination into long time Conservative principles. McRae, ever a man of the future, pushed for change and a party breakthrough: a first national convention in the west. Not without considerable debate, it finally was decided the meeting would be held in Winnipeg in the fall.

Not only did McRae push for a western convention, he also scouted the ranks to identify those most likely to contend the leadership. He soon selected R.B. Bennett, a native of New Brunswick but a resident of Calgary since 1897, as the best choice. Bennett, however, wasn't everybody's favourite. He was a big, burly man of 57, an always fastidiously dressed bachelor who some felt was too much of a cold fish to lead the party. As a lawyer, he had many influential contacts in the business world where, like McRae, he had made considerable wealth from land speculation and other commercial ventures. He was ambitious, autocratic, and an untiring worker. He also had an uncontrollable sweet tooth, consumed six meals a day, and eventually paid for his sins by becoming grossly overweight and developing diabetes.

McRae was conference organizer. There were few who would argue it was not extremely well planned down to the last detail, but he riled some with his open support of Bennett. One newspaper reported that there were complaints about the "steam roller" tactics used by Bennett and his supporters. Between them, McRae and Bennett had the money to fill the smoked-filled backrooms. The very close tie between the organizer and a candidate was unusual—these were unusual times for the Conservatives who were smarting from too many defeats and were desperate to find a winner.

The success of the Winnipeg gathering was almost solely McRae's work. In less than six months he built a new more efficient party machine, helped ensure the right delegates would be in attendance at Winnipeg, stopped squabbles, tossed out unwise resolutions, and threw his support behind the ultimate winner, R.B. Bennett. Before the convention began he had calculated exactly how the leadership vote would go, and his assessment was deadly accurate. Bennett emerged as an easy winner, taking 780 votes to win on the second ballot, far in front of his nearest competitor, interim leader Hugh Guthrie, who polled only 320 votes. What pleased the convention was that they had elected a new leader without any major splits, divisions, or anger that was likely to last. As one paper noted, "McRae was given the greatest personal ovation of the meeting. A resolution thanking him for his work brought forth a demand for a speech from him. He modestly declined and then was serenaded by a lusty rendition of 'For he's a jolly good fellow.'"

The *Province* claimed that Bennett's win was one of the greatest political victories Canada had known: a radical departure from the past and—at last—some recognition for the west. It poured on the praise, asserting that "all through the convention the west has been triumphant and one figure from the west coast, General A.D. McRae is recognized as among those chiefly responsible for the success. As chairman of the organizing committee he is credited with accomplishing wonders. His ovation yesterday afternoon was one of the most demonstrable personal tributes conceivable." Robert Reade wrote that he wasn't holding a stopwatch, but enthusiastically reported that "the convention cheered McRae for half-an-hour," at least.

In the ensuing months McRae became a more prominent figure on Parliament Hill. The general's forward march took a tumble there though on March 12, 1928. That evening McRae was leaving The Hill with six or seven colleagues when he slipped on a patch of ice near the main gate and slammed his head to the ground. He was rushed to hospital with what were described as serious injuries. The *Ottawa Journal* gave front-page coverage to the accident and his critical medical condition, noting that a dinner he had planned for Bennett on March 14 had now been cancelled. McRae's elderly mother Mary in Glencoe heard of his injury and said she instinctively knew that he had suffered a severe concussion. She quickly travelled to his Ottawa bedside where she conferred with his doctor who confirmed her fears. She said she had seen the lines of his fractured skull in a dream. A week later there were signs McRae's condition was improving; however, a news report said, "he likely will be away from Parliament for about six weeks where he will be greatly missed as one of its most distinguished figures." This was outstanding recognition for a rookie member. By March 20, readers were told that although he had fractured his skull his injuries were not as bad as originally feared and, typically, McRae was "chaffing at his inaction."

The man from Hycroft had been so good at the job of organizing the convention that the caucus almost immediately named him chief party organizer. He was totally different from any of his predecessors in this position. He had all the assurance of a self-made man, was ignorant of orthodox party strategy, and was convinced that business and military tactics could be applied successfully in politics. His reputation in business and industry now helped him as a bagman to raise funds for the party. He was extremely effective in this role, knowing exactly what he wanted and how to get it. And he had no qualms about being dictatorial; it was a trait he had learned in the army.

He opened an office at 140 Wellington Street near Parliament Hill, hired staff, and shook up the organization by asking all MPs and candidates for basic statistics and facts about their ridings. Surprisingly, this was something that had never been done before. He travelled the country and visited each riding, sometimes with Bennett, sometimes alone. McRae's budget of $25,000 gave him the power to do what was needed. It gave him leeway to give money to those who needed it for campaigning, and he probably dipped into his own and Bennett's fortunes when there was an established need to do so. He made nearly as many enemies as he made friends, however, because he was sometimes efficiently ruthless in getting rid of those who were not suitable candidates. At the outset some old party members doubted they had chosen the right man. McRae went on organizing in his own way though, and the doubters finally couldn't argue with success.

While setting up the information ministry in England, McRae was credited with having revolutionized British ideas about national advertising. He applied some of these ideas in organizing for the 1930 Canadian election. In no time he had 40 women working to turn out campaign material and distribute it across the country. Using a technique new to electioneering, he arranged to put messages from candidates on radio. Old-timers argued that the victory would still depend on personal campaigning in barbers' shops, local stores, and on doorsteps—McRae's strategy was a new approach, a new program he drafted on behalf of Bennett and his party. He felt it was needed to get the voters' attention as they suffered from the increasing effects of the 1929 Wall Street market crash and the developing Depression that was spreading across North America.

One Ottawa correspondent wrote, "Though the main laurels of victory may be placed on another's head, a special medal will certainly be struck for McRae as the organizer of victory. In the last three years he is credited with having constructed the most efficient electioneering mechanism known in the history of Canada. He will not be highly visible and out front beating the big drum in the 1930 Conservative election campaign, but it will nonetheless dance to the tune of the powerful man from the west."

McRae denied that he was known as the "supreme generalissimo" of the Tories' election fighting force. He frequently said he wanted to stay out of the limelight: "I don't count. Our whole campaign turns around our leader Mr. Bennett. It is his principles and personality we are putting before the public."

"Canada first, last and all the time."

Two of McRae's major interests in his one term as Member of Parliament were the future of the troubled sockeye fishing industry on the Pacific coast and his advocacy of a more scientific approach to its problems—a prescient view in light of today's coho and sockeye shortages. Once again it appears he was far ahead of his time, foreseeing the future with great clarity.

He said that if research didn't improve, museums soon would be the only place to see a sockeye salmon. He also pushed once again for a major drive by government to populate and develop the Peace River district, which he insisted would add wealth to the B.C. and Canadian economies and sharply increase the number of people in Western Canada. This was a proposal based on his experience in helping colonize Saskatchewan and Alberta 30 years earlier. He envisioned a booming B.C. Interior region that would be home to more than two million people. His ideas were not developed, even partially, for many years.

His praise for Canada, its future, and his pride and patriotism were stated strongly in Parliament and in a letter to his constituents.

> The cover on the copy of a speech I made in Parliament on June 6, 1929, and sent to voters best summed up my fears for the future of the sockeye salmon industry in B.C. It stated that in 1905

fishermen and cannery workers produced 1,080,673 cases of sockeye. In 1928 this had slumped to 202,542 cases. The figures speak for themselves of the increasing plight of the industry, more and more fishermen and cannery workers are unemployed, and an even bigger disaster is coming unless we take strong steps to remedy the situation. It is urgent that we achieve the results and efficiencies of the Americans along the Pacific coast in their fishing industry. I told them that I intended to apply for an annual, parliamentary vote for money to be applied to a continuing program to clean out our barren rivers and stock our spawning grounds with different varieties of salmon so that the fishing season will be as long as possible. A fixed and steady program extended over five years will provide a great deal of work for the fishermen in this district during the off season. I am also convinced that if we adopt modern methods such as those which have so effectively restored the Columbia River, we will have, as soon as the four-year cycle can come around, an increasing supply of salmon in rivers that now produce little or no fish at all. This program, if carried out consistently and immediately, I believe will soon increase the fish supply along the coast to three or four times its recent size.

I advocate the appointment of a five-man commission, representing, for example, fishermen, cannery men and businessmen, all serving without pay, to look at the fish culture developments which have worked so well in Oregon. I point to the fact that our previous scientific work, on which we have spent a lot of money in the last 55 years, has resulted in the fish getting less. The United States has done much better. There was the Columbia comeback in 1928, a year in which we spent $112, 532.65 on the work, a little less than in the United States, but with much less result. And it has to be remembered that there the project was sustained by the industry. Our Department of Marine and Fisheries can not grasp the situation in B.C., their efforts have been feeble. I do agree with the provision of a three-plane air patrol over B.C. waters costing $40,000 to safeguard our industry and watch the increasing number of American boats which are using B.C. ports much more extensively.

I oppose the plan to spend money on a fishing museum in Prince Rupert. We already have several in different places in B.C. although I am beginning to fear that we have about reached the stage of the fisheries problem in our province where museums will be necessary in order to display the last specimens of that great commercial fish, the sockeye salmon.

I also am concerned about the power that is held by the three American representatives on the group dealing with the new international treaty salmon industry in the Fraser River. This must be examined very carefully or I fear the time will come when the Americans could have a vested interest in this area.

I believe with all my heart that the development of the Peace River country would be one of the greatest boons to British Columbia and to all of Canada. It is a mighty region with a great many resources and could be a breadbasket for an increasingly more peopled world. Without being too unkind to my colleagues, I recently made an extensive trip through the area, something that can't be done with a Parliamentary railway pass. In a month I covered some 1,500 miles backpacking by horse, on foot and paddling along rivers. I travelled some of the same routes as Alexander McKenzie took when he explored the area in 1789. I interviewed some 250 to 300 people, including merchants, traders, trappers, Indians and old timers. They told me of the love, confidence, hope and aspirations they have for this majestic and sweeping area. I have studied the Peace River country, garnering the best scientific and agricultural advice from many experts, and I make it all available to all who are interested in the future of this vast region, larger than many of the countries of Europe.

I have had assessments made down to the cost of clearing land that would provide excellent farms for the people I believe we should assist in moving into the Peace River country as settlers, particularly those from the British Isles. The potential of the area certainly would keep the boys home on the farm, unlike those like myself who had to leave at an early age to find opportunities. Even if we spent as much as $50 million in the future to bring people in, we would be richly rewarded. This Peace River country of B.C. could easily become home to more than two million people. We need more positive thinking from the government and our immigration officials, some of whom seem to living in 1890 and not 1929.

I want the constituents to know that the government of Mackenzie King and his Liberals has been very slow in tackling the country's problems. The most recent budget was a "raise more money" budget. It offered little relief for the average man and woman. Our attempt to have the sales tax removed was turned down, even a subsequent bid to have them at least take it off boots, shoes and clothing. I told them that imaginative new industrial projects along with development of the Peace River would benefit all of B.C. resulting in a million people living around Burrard Inlet.

I believe as Canadians we are second to no people in the world that we are big enough and able enough to look after ourselves and to run our own business. I object particularly to the attitude of some of our people who seem to have that "inferiority complex" which says hush, hush, let us wait and see what the other fellow is going to do to us.

It is my humble judgment that we spend entirely too much of our time trying to help run the affairs of other countries of the world instead of looking after Canada. We are a young, virile nation with very many challenges of our own sufficient to occupy all of our time.

Today no country is more desirable than Canada, no country has greater opportunities. We are told very frequently about the "great resources with which a generous Providence has endowed us." My suggestion is that we adopt a national policy of development which will enable us to enjoy some of this great endowment while we yet live. Let us get back to first principles; Canada first, last and all the time.

McRae had lived in the United States, started on the road to business success in the state of Minnesota and married there, and yet he remained ever the Canadian nationalist. This was one of his most fervent assertions.

Man of Terrific Energy

Gratton O'Leary, an Ottawa parliamentary correspondent, was very impressed with A.D. McRae when he met him on Parliament Hill prior to the 1930 election. He wrote one lengthy story with pictures about McRae.

Sam Hughes made more than his share of mistakes before he was fired as Canada's top military man in the first great war, but one of the things he did right was talking Vancouver's Alexander Duncan McRae into joining the militia before the guns began to boom. The millionaire industrialist from B.C. had an uncanny capacity for getting the right men to do the right things. He fulfilled his first job of horse buying with efficiency and without the graft that tainted similar dealings elsewhere. His organizational ability led him to the rank of Quartermaster General in charge of supply and transportation for the forces in France, and before the war ended he was asked by the British to help them organize their first ministry of information and promoted to the rank of major general.

Restless after the war, his money made and with his 1914 decision to sever direct connections with the industrial empire he had built, McRae decided to get into B.C. politics. A disgruntled Tory he formed his own Provincial Party and launched an attempt to build a new Jerusalem on the Pacific coast. As more than one politician has learned, creating a new Jerusalem is no easy task. When the dust had settled, the Provincial Party elected exactly three members and McRae went down to personal defeat. Sadder but wiser, he went back to the Conservative Party, although there were diehard B.C. Tories who detested him for this to the end of their days.

The Tories knew McRae had funds to run a good campaign and he was successful in being nominated in what was seen as a very tough fight in North Vancouver in the 1926 federal election. He won, but the Tory party lost to Mackenzie King's Liberals and was in disarray. Mindful of McRae's reputation as an organizer and manager, they made him the chairman for their 1927 leadership convention in a desperate search for a new chief.

In this 1930 election campaign McRae operates out in the open—different from his Liberal counterpart, Andrew Haydon—and delights in hurling himself against the enemy in frontal attacks. He loves crowds, loves to mingle with people, and seemingly enthuses in getting into the constituency to meet the 'boys.' He knows every politician and correspondent in Ottawa by their first names wants to make friends with them and insists on entertaining them. McRae has thrown bigger parties than any other political organizer in Ottawa for three or four decades.

Starting almost from scratch, in three years he has built up an amazing propaganda machine with all the equipment and ingenuity to sell a political party to the public at large. The Conservative headquarters resembles one of those publicity and propaganda bureaus found in connection with vast research foundations in the United States.

McRae, curiously enough, is far from being formidable in parliament. The truth is that General

McRae's genius has seemingly more to do with political organization than with political statesmanship. Of this, however, McRae seems to be fairly conscious. Too keen and too able to fool himself, he knows that his ideas about government are not excessive and that his personality and style of oratory are not of the kind that sways or persuades crowds. It is this knowledge, plus a concentration upon the job of staging the management of things and of watching from the wings the actors he puts on the stage that makes him so successful.

He is an engaging form. He has a cheery optimistic word for everyone and is seldom ruffled. His friends praise his loyalty, swear that they would bank upon him or with him, and that at all times and in all places he is the very best of comrades. Clever enough to be cynical, McRae conceals his cynicism. And while sometimes some in his party have chafed under his tendency to be autocratic, he is trusted to a greater degree than most party organizers and exercises much the same authority as a general over the officers of his division.

Like all successful organizers, McRae has tremendous energy. For weeks and months on end he worked almost 20 out of 24 hours in getting ready for the Winnipeg convention. Last summer when most Canadian millionaires were vacationing in Europe or at Canada's sea sides, McRae was going up and down the country interviewing party workers, farmers, workingmen, businessmen and party lieutenants. Last summer he completed the task of visiting all of the 245 ridings in the Dominion.

McRae overlooked nothing and neglected nothing that could contribute to his party's ultimate victory. He also set himself the task of persuading whatever else was left of the population by the more indirect methods of publicity and propaganda. He employed cunning writers to turn out handbooks and leaflets and he flooded the land with them. What the effect of it all is we shall see.

If General McRae puts Honourable R.B. Bennett on the prime minister's throne, the likelihood is that he will have his reward. And the most likely reward, if the inspired voices be right will be the Canadian High Commissionership in London, a post presently vacant but soon to be occupied by Vincent Massey. General McRae would like that; and as he has wealth, business experience, organizing power, and knows London and the English, he would competently fill the job.

McRae mingled freely and frequently with the Ottawa press gallery, quickly learning their names and the papers they represented. He often joked with them about their likes and dislikes. He had a genial friendly manner at public gatherings; it was an approach honed to perfection in meetings with employees, business associates, politicians, and royalty. Yet he often admitted he much preferred to relax and socialize in a more private setting with those he knew well, in the homes of friends, or at the lavish parties held in the opulent surroundings of his own design at Hycroft.

The Marvelous Masked Balls

The social whirl became a whirlpool. Dances, teas, receptions kept the big houses filled to the doors and sparkling with lights. Yachts glided over Coal Harbour and English Bay. The Edwardian Age had come to town, and the young folk broke loose, evoking the tut-tuts of their elders. Visiting aristocrats were submerged in champagne and debutantes; there were reigning belles, and here and there emerged a new species, the playboy, like "Afternoon Tea Charlie" Henshaw, who convulsed a yachting party and scandalized the town by providing his guests with bathing dresses straight from Paris—which disintegrated after ten minutes in the water. Ladies sat on stools in the shops to be waited on by polite clerks and never carried a parcel too big to slip into their purses. Charming girls swung in hammocks on summer lawns, or sang "The Trail of the Lonesome Pine" in the dusk at beach picnics; mandolins tinkled on front porches in the evenings, and rag-time tunes drifted down the streets.

Oh!—It was a wonderful, wonderful time.

—From the chapter "The Golden Years" in
Vancouver Milltown to Metropolis by Alan Morley

The golden years were the time when the McRae girls were growing up, but Peggy's wedding marked the start of the high life at Hycroft. Blaunche McRae loved to entertain, and once her girls were all married and living away from home, she concentrated her energies on designing elaborate parties that became the toast of the town no matter what the season. Her husband had entered politics, so strategy meetings were held at the house and constituency parties were thrown regularly for movers and shakers in the political arena. Sometimes there were charity fund-raising events, or there might be a spur of the moment party to meet a new face or hear a new speaker. There were teas on the terrace or in the rose garden on summer afternoons. On winter weekends there were dances and dinners—some small, some large—each one graciously hosted by the McRaes. One Shaughnessy matron commented many years later that an invitation from Blaunche McRae, even if it arrived a little late, was like a command performance. It was considered an honour and a pleasure to visit Hycroft. The most famous parties, however, the ones that generated the biggest newspaper stories, and the ones that everyone wanted to attend were the New Year's Eve fancy dress masquerade balls.

Guests were provided with a theme for the evening two months before the event so that costumes could be created in time for New Year's Eve when everyone arrived dressed as the invitation decreed. Each year visitors were transported into an elaborate setting from the past, recreated by their hostess Blaunche McRae. In later years invitations were limited to about 100, but on occasion as many as 400 costumed friends attended dinner, danced, or partook of a bowl of consommé—the traditional farewell service before guests departed in the wee small hours of New Year's Day. There was frequently more than one overnight houseguest after the ball. Even the gardener was always on special duty New Year's Eve, ensuring the pool house was locked up so no one could fall in; once or twice he fished an inebriated guest out of the circular pond beneath the fountain in the courtyard.

From November onward, the ladies of Shaughnessy compared notes to see who had been invited, and what each was going to wear. One newspaper reported, "Anticipated since November when the invitations were issued, members of the younger set have been arranging charming and original costumes in which to appear and the results of their choice were seen in

Each New Year's Eve during the 1920s and 1930s the ballroom at Hycroft came alive with a fancy dress ball, where the grandest costumes were often worn by the host and hostess. Sometimes the party began with dinner, but often it began much later, and ended only when consommé was served just before guests departed the next morning. It was always an event to be remembered.

the bewildering array of old-world dresses, fantastic dancing costumes and beautiful stiff brocades glittering with golden embroidery and scintillating with jewels. The big ballroom of Hycroft proved a setting of beauty for the maze of dancers; ancient met modern as a medieval grande dame waltzed with man-about-town; and Columbine and harlequin pirouetted in the corner."

The McRae's closest friends, well-known business associates, and the occasional politician were invited to the New Year's Eve dances. Most of the regular guests were long-term friends and they made up a list of who's who in Vancouver at that time: the Eric Hambers, the Malkins, the Abbotts, the Spencers, the Woodwards, the Bell-Irvings, the Boultbees, the James

McMullens, and Mrs. J. W. Stewart. Over the years thousands of people attended the New Year's parties, and the McRaes greeted each one by name.

And always there were flowers, a little different each year, ranging from palms and shaggy pink chrysanthemums to poinsettias. Often at this season of the year the twelve fireplaces at Hycroft were decorated with evergreen boughs filled with twinkling green, red, and yellow Christmas lights. During one masquerade ball Blaunche McRae created a carnival where dinner was served at small tables placed throughout the main downstairs rooms and hallway. Outside, the gardens were ablaze with lights that outlined the pool, fountain, and all the trees surrounding the courtyard.

On the eve of 1927 the theme was famous couples, and at one point during the evening when a Shakespearian king (Alexander Duncan McRae) asked a young cowgirl (his daughter Blanche) to dance, everyone laughed because the costumes were so incompatible and looked incongruous together. Blanche's costume that year was a short white satin skirt with a white silk fringe; she wore silver slippers, a red tie and sash, and a broad-brimmed white felt hat.

One year, guests were transported to the Orient. All the decorations were in red and gold. Hycroft was described on the newspaper's social pages as "a mass of colour and brightness as would captivate the heart of even the highest-born Oriental prince or princess. In the circular driveway that surrounds the marble pond, red, yellow, and green lights were intertwined to form a great circle of radiance while playing on the pond itself and sparkling in the water that falls from the fountain statue were powerful red reflectors. Guests were received in the red-carpeted reception hall complete with red silk plush and old gold furniture. Mrs. Victor Spencer as an Oriental dancer wore one of the brightest costumes ever recalled in gold and flame satin with a headdress of ostrich feathers and she wore gold shoes with turned up toes."

On one occasion Blaunche McRae's costume was particularly elaborate; although there was never a plain one. She dressed as

Queen Elizabeth the First and wore a jade green and gold brocade gown with a white velvet panel in front, embroidered with pearls and diamonds. It was adorned with an Elizabethan ruff made of rose-point lace that fell to her waist. She even wore a red velvet crown outlined with gold, and she carried a sceptre. Alexander McRae's matching costume was made of black and white satin and velvet. He was a distinguished gentleman of the Elizabethan period: a role he played with relish.

Blaunche's mother, Mama Howe, frequently arrived from Minneapolis for the Christmas holiday season and always got into the spirit of the evening by appearing in a costume that she had specially prepared to match the theme of the evening. There were often Italian dancing girls,

Blaunche McRae, dressed as Queen Elizabeth the First in a jade green and gold brocade gown, is pictured on the main staircase at Hycroft, with one of the family dogs sitting at her feet. On the wall behind her is one of the murals that originally adorned many of the walls in the mansion.

Spanish dancing girls, and gypsies. Anyone attending the dance could easily meet a woman of the desert or see the yellow tartan costume of a Columbine. Mrs. Foster Huntting was attired one year as "Night" in a costume made of midnight-blue satin and tulle with stars and half moons encrusted with diamanté.

One of the McRaes' friends, Fanta Verchere, commented, "The New Year's Eve parties were the best of all. Mrs. Howe was usually there and she was quite a character. There was a rumour she had once been a bare-back rider in a circus but that doesn't seem likely. She always stood out in a crowd though because unlike the other older women she didn't let her hair go grey. It always remained dark and there weren't many women who dyed their hair in those days." She also remembered the wonderful food the McRaes served and the lateness of the parties, which sometimes carried on until five in the morning when the hot bouillon was served before the drive home. She said, "Even when short-skirts came in with the flapper style, the men still wore white tie and tails, and I remember how dashing and distinguished they all looked."

In 1928 all of McRae's daughters and their husbands were home for a mid-winter visit and had a wonderful time together on New Year's Eve. Blanche and Richard Baker came dressed as Indian chiefs: Richard was wearing black and white with Blanche in red and white and both donning white feather headdresses. Peggy was in from New York, dressed as a Hawaiian maiden in silver, and Lucile had driven up from Seattle for the party, bringing with her a powder-blue bluebird costume. One of the papers that year said, "No more brilliant affair is given in the city than the annual fancy dress ball held at Hycroft by General and Mrs. A. D. McRae."

New Year's Eve 1929 was by all accounts one of the most spectacular parties of all. The theme was Spanish, and the ballroom at Hycroft was transformed into a Spanish court. According to newspaper accounts everyone came "dressed to the nines" and there were Spanish grandees and dons with their ladies, as well as toreadors and matadors in shining red capes. Blaunche had carefully recreated the atmosphere of old Spain, and the costumes of the host and hostess were copied from figures in famous paintings by Valesquez. Their daughter Blanche wore a costume made to resemble one of Urban's famous "Follies" gowns. The skirt was made of taffeta ruffles ranging from shades of pale peach at the bottom up to darker rose-orange near the waist; under each shaded ruffle, roses peeked out of the folds. She also wore a huge black Spanish hat with matching roses under the brim. Lucile, who was home for Christmas and New Year, dressed in a beautiful white Spanish shawl that was embroidered and deeply fringed in green.

Despite the crash of 1929, which must have affected McRae's fortunes to some extent, the arrival of 1930 was marked in well-established Hycroft style. The theme was the 1,001 Legends of the Arabian Nights. Blaunche McRae was a Persian lady and Alexander was resplendent as a shah in a white satin blouse and black velvet tunic over many-coloured striped pantaloons. Blanche Baker was an East Indian princess and Lucile Paul an Egyptian, like one of the figures carved on the walls in the Valley of the Kings. The masquerade ball was described on the social pages as "beyond doubt, the most brilliant social function of the season and an inspiration for a great many interesting pre-dinner parties and informal entertaining at lovely homes all over the city before it began. There must have been dozens of pre-ball parties, and the guests started arriving about 10 p.m. but were still coming until nearly mid-night." The social scene in Vancouver was changing; the city was growing up, and the times were more serious and less carefree. The city's growing sophistication was showing.

Gradually, the big balls faded away. When McRae lost his seat in Parliament, the need for he and his wife to entertain politicians and party stalwarts was greatly reduced, so they returned to their preferred style with smaller gatherings of close friends. The economic downturn of the 1930s also influenced the style of entertaining for the entire decade.

The Little Girl
from the Kitchen Remembers

The parties and entertaining at Hycroft were a part of the McRae world, but there was another group "downstairs" in the house that was very much a part of their lifestyle. For one little girl who entered the house for the first time as a youngster it was an entrancing and exciting new world.

Betty Youngson Ingram was only ten years old when she first saw Hycroft. Her mother had been hired to manage the kitchen, and for all the time her mother was employed there, Betty spent most weekends with her. In a letter that rests in the archives at Hycroft, she recalled her wonderous days in the huge house on the hill.

When I was only ten, my mother Jessie Ann Youngson was hired as cook for the McRae family. She had been recommended for the job by Uncle Alex McTavish who was one of the owners of the Patisserie Parisienne Bakery on Granville near 12th where Mrs. McRae sometimes shopped. We were newly arrived from the highlands of Scotland in the autumn of 1925, trying to establish ourselves in the city and while my father Bill had a job in Woodward's garage, the job for mother with the McRae's meant we would be able to move out of Uncle Alex's house and have a place of our own much sooner.

The McRaes entertained a lot, generally giving lavish parties on weekends and one of mother's terms of employment was that she live-in at Hycroft on weekends and have her time off on less busy days. Mrs. McRae realized mother was unhappy at leaving me with my aunt all the time when I was out of school and said I would be welcome to spend weekends at Hycroft. I was delighted with the suggestion and mother said I could come providing I did not make a nuisance of myself. For me it was a relief to get away from my three screaming cousins who seemed to fight constantly. Whenever there was a simple task I could do I helped mother and other times I read or did puzzles.

I ate with the large staff at Hycroft and we took our meals together in a small dining room off the kitchen. The butler's name was Mr. Fleck, a thin lanky man a little like Fred Astaire who always wore a black suit with long coat-tails. He looked after the silverware and glasses in the pantry and frequently purchased wine and other spirits for General McRae. The chauffeur, Mr. Grey, teased me unmercifully because he said he liked to see me blush and the gardener's name was Mr. McDonald. He kept the grounds immaculately with hardly a blade of grass out of place.

There were many things I could do to help mother. When they were in season I shelled peas and often took the skins off blanched almonds or seeded raisins with a sharp knife and sometimes I stirred a sauce while mother attended to other things in the kitchen.

We settled into a routine and I always looked forward to my weekends at Hycroft. Dad took me to McRae Avenue every Friday evening and left me at the tall wrought-iron gates. I went through the small side gate, passed the fountain and the rose garden to the back of the house where a door led to a small hallway and the back stairs. I would run as quietly as I could up all three flights to mother's bedroom where it was always warm and comfortable. She had a private very elegant built-in bathtub and to me it was the height of luxury to soak in warm water with a cake of ivory soap that actually floated. I had never seen one before. The towels were large and thick and I almost disappeared when I was wrapped in one. It made me feel pampered to experience such luxury.

The food was delicious, all of it prepared by my mother who took special pains to ensure it was artistically presented and the staff ate very similar meals to the family unless there was a special banquet or the General was throwing a stag party as he often did. When everything had been cleared away and the guests had gone home, General McRae always came into the kitchen and thanked mother for her efforts. He gave credit where credit was due and as a result mother kept a very high standard and worked with a happy heart.

Each morning at 10 a.m. Mrs. McRae came to the kitchen to discuss the day's menus with mother. Then down to the cellar she would go to check supplies in the larder.

The three daughters in the McRae family were Blanche, Lucile and Margaret who was called Peggy. She loved animals and had three Great Dane dogs that slept on big Hudson's Bay woollen blankets—grey ones with black points—in a closet adjoining her bedroom. The dogs were very large and I was a little fearful of them. I thought they looked more like horses from the stable than dogs and three of them together could do a lot of damage. Peggy was the youngest and her sisters said she was spoiled, but she had a lot of fun and always seemed happy and carefree. She married a man named Walter Seligman who was from New York and their wedding was one of the grandest affairs ever held at Hycroft. It took place on a Monday so I was back at school and didn't see it but mother and the others filled me in and back at my aunt's house we read about it in the papers.

When Lucile had her baby, a sweet little girl, she returned to Hycroft for a while and hired a nanny to look after the baby while she was there. The nanny was Miss Muirhead and sometimes she let me hold the baby. Lucile and her husband lived in Seattle.

Another visitor, at least once a year, was Mrs. Howe, Mrs. McRae's mother. Everyone called her "Mamma Howe." For an older lady she was very slim and agile and I always remember the breakfast she had each morning—two raw eggs in a glass with a jigger of brandy. To me it looked revolting.

She generally came for Christmas and New Year and the celebrations were unforgettable. For the staff it was a busy time. It took days to decorate the house which was transformed into a fairyland of glitter. There was not just one tree, but several beautifully festooned evergreens in various rooms on the main floor. The one I remember most vividly was in the entrance hall at the bottom of the grand staircase. On Christmas morning Mrs. McRae took me by the hand and led me to the base of the tree. We stood together looking at it, shining in all its glory and decorated with delicate blown-glass birds with real feather tails. In all my life I had never seen anything as lovely. Mrs. McRae reached under the tree and brought out the most beautiful doll I'd ever seen. She told me Santa Claus had left it for me when he called during the night. It was so lovely I couldn't believe it was for me. The doll had blonde curls, long eye-lashes, a pink silk dress and a fur-trimmed velvet cape. I was almost speechless with surprise but was able to stammer

out "Thank you very much Mrs. McRae for the beautiful doll."
It was inadequate I knew, but I think she understood my
bewilderment. For many years it was my most prized
possession.

I saw the dining room that same morning, set for Christmas
dinner and decorated in shimmering white and silver from the
candelabra right down to the smallest salt dish. Fresh flowers
were everywhere, most of them beautiful white narcissus and
the air was filled with their sweet perfume.

The kitchen was the busiest room of all that day, humming
with activity and filled with the wonderful smells that identified
the treats to be served at dinner. This was truly a Christmas
feast, with stuffed turkey and a glazed and decorated ham.
There was also a magnificent very large prime rib roast to be
available for nighttime snacks later on. General McRae always
enjoyed carving the meat and made quite a ceremony out of
it.

Dessert was a delightful experience and included the
traditional plum pudding and hard sauce well laced with rum
and shaped into fancy forms as well as English trifle, tarts and
short bread.

It was a happy gathering of family and friends who arrived
for dinner and more guests appeared later for the dancing and
a grand party that followed in the ballroom. Many toasts were
drunk and Mr. Fleck the butler told mother that one had been
said in appreciation of her cooking. A group of musicians had
been hired for the after-dinner dancing and the wine flowed
freely, the ladies gowns rustled and gleamed and I was told the
house echoed with the sound of music and laughter, though I
was sound asleep upstairs in bed. When all the guests left
snowflakes were falling to add to the splendour of a perfect
Christmas day. The next morning Mamma Howe had four raw
eggs with a jigger of brandy.

Noble Sacrifice?

There were reminders of the First World War when McRae resolutely decided to fight the 1930 general election on a grand strategic basis from Ottawa, where he would have instant knowledge of campaign developments across Canada and control of the party's program. Tory foot soldiers in North Vancouver would have to do the frontline battling for him in his own riding. With a worsening economic situation across Canada and in all parts of the industrialized world, Prime Minister Mackenzie King made a newspaper announcement on May 6 that there would be a fall general election, the date to be given later. This news took second place on the *Vancouver Sun's* front page to a story that former Vernon schoolboy Walter Henry Hickman had won the Vice-Regal Medal as the best of the University of B.C.'s 229 graduating students. On May 30, when King dropped the other shoe, he said voting day would be earlier than he had first indicated—July 28—not in the fall, but in summer. It was a strange choice for a general election date—but King took advice from unusual sources.

R.B. Bennett opened the Tory campaign symbolically in Winnipeg, the scene of his ascension to the party throne. McRae and other party leaders knew the west would be a major battleground and they would have to make gains there if they hoped to win. In the previous Parliament the Conservatives held only one of the prairie seats, while in B.C. they took twelve of fourteen, one of them held by McRae. The Depression was affecting western farmers badly and the Conservatives believed it could be fertile ground for growth from those unhappy with

King and his policies. They were also banking on the fact that Bennett was a westerner to draw support. The opening rally in Winnipeg was promising, attracting a huge crowd of 7,000 people. Bennett's address was heard coast-to-coast on radio. This was McRae's innovation, and it was dubbed "the greatest national broadcast ever."

McRae's ability to accurately gauge the future was a boon for his party. He had watched the growing importance of radio broadcasts in American election campaigns and knew that in the years ahead it would be just as important to Canadian politicians. He determined that radio should be used as much as possible, even though many Canadians were still without wireless sets. The Conservative slogan "Give Canada a Chance" was heard frequently on the airwaves.

While promising some trade protection, Bennett emphasized he would mount an aggressive campaign to support the marketing of Canadian goods in the face of increasing protectionism in other countries around the world. During the campaign, Australia clamped huge tariffs of up to 200 percent on B.C. lumber, effectively killing exports to that country and affecting the profits of Western Canada Lumber where McRae still held a big block of shares. In Regina, where 1,500 unemployed demanded something be done to get them jobs, Bennett promised he would get Canadian goods to market "or fall out of power."

Battling back against claims he was powerless to do anything about the Depression's increasingly crippling effects, a windy and buoyant Mackenzie King drew 9,000 Liberal loyalists to his meeting in Vancouver. They roared their support, and only a few left early despite the prime minister's incredible two and three-quarter-hour speech—long even for this era of marathon performances. King said a new Liberal government would fight its way out of the current economic morass. He slammed Bennett's trade policies as unworkable and unrealistic, and copied a McRae platform—a rail link to the Peace River country and the development of this huge relatively untouched area—as one of his own election promises.

On June 16, the *Province* reported that the financial situation was getting worse by the day, with the New York Stock Exchange losing billions in its biggest fall since November 1929. It told its readers that when Bennett hit town he poured out the party line "before more than 7,000 in Western Canada's greatest city, sitting on the shores of the harbour through which the grain of his adopted home (Calgary) pours to the world." There was a chance the pour might become a trickle, but despite pessimistic newspaper reports, everybody hoped for the best.

On July 1, the *Province* reported that the city had spent $337,240 out of its annual $500,000 budget for relief, and more unemployed were heading west from across the country. The story stated there had already been reports of graft and kickbacks in the city's relief department in the supply of meal tickets to those desperately in need.

While many were out of work, there still were many employed, and nothing stopped the annual staff summer picnics staged by the two big department stores: the Hudson's Bay Company and Spencer's Stores Ltd. The steamers *Lady Alexandra* and *Lady Cecilia* were both called into service to transport 1,500 people to the daylong events that were both staged in Sechelt on the Sunshine Coast north of Vancouver. The papers reported that the Hudson's Bay picnic honoured the store's oldest employee, Fred Herbert, who had been with the company 34 years, and men in plus fours and berets competed with their wives in a needle threading contest. At the Spencer's Stores picnic, Fred Weaver and his orchestra tootled for dancing on the *Lady Alexandra*, while Arthur Delamont and 25 boys from General Gordon School entertained on the *Lady Cecilia*. Store owner Victor Spencer was a catcher on one of the softball games, and Miss Halliwell of the parcel department was the mystery Orphan Annie who was appropriately uncovered by Ron Ray of the delivery department. The same day back in Vancouver sprinter Percy Williams, who won the gold medal at the 1928 Olympics, was beaten in a race at Hastings Park by American Eddie Tolan, despite recording his best time ever of 10:35 seconds for the 100-metre sprint.

McRae, guiding the national campaign from Ottawa thousands of miles away, heard ominous news from the home front in his own North Vancouver riding: His absence was under attack from opponents and the Liberal press. The *Province* put the best shine on his use of "vulcanite discs" to get his message to constituents. As the use of radio had become more familiar and increased in popularity, McRae had urged people across the country to organize "radio parties" and listen to messages by Bennett. Not everyone had a radio, nor could afford one. Some newspaper advertisements showed a top model radio set "complete with tubes" at a pricey $325, although there were cheaper ones. By comparison a Ford roadster or sedan cost $520 and $598. McRae cut his records in Ottawa and sent them to the coast where workers organized gatherings to listen to his gramophone messages. A *Province* editorial said they helped produce brevity of speech, although there was no opportunity for the art of heckling.

The *Sun* took swipes at McRae's absence. It noted he was "playing ringmaster in the East and the Canadian people, those fine Britishers in North Vancouver, will resent it." The editorial went on to criticize his wealth and dubbed him "an absentee landlord," adding, "General McRae must have great confidence in his Victor Talking Machine Company when he thinks that the prestige of his money will defeat that fine Canadian, Mr. Munn. He must have great contempt for the people of North Vancouver if he thinks they can be bought and sold like slaves when he stays in Ottawa playing politics and reporting to his constituents by phonograph." These comments reflected the focus of both the Liberal Party and the climate of the time that was suspicious of newfangled contraptions.

McRae wasn't bothered by the Liberal paper's attacks, but the bad news arrived when the nominations for candidates closed. North Vancouver was going to be a two-way fight between McRae and the Liberals' A.E. Munn, a well-known lumberman who had been an MLA in Victoria from 1924 to 1928. McRae had won in 1926 on a split vote, the Labour candidate taking away what would otherwise have been Liberal votes. No one knew better than he the danger of a straight fight, but there was some hope that enough voters might find Mackenzie King's efforts to cope with the Depression so awful that McRae could hang onto his seat.

Just before voting day, the *Vancouver Sun* confidently reported that Mackenzie King was well on his way to a smashing victory. Taking a poke at the opposition party's strategy, the paper contended that the "blame for the obvious collapse of the Conservative campaign is placed on McRae." But the *Sun* was wrong; on July 28 the voters produced a major upset and western Canada got its first prime minister. Conservatives across the country were ecstatic as they welcomed a new government led by R.B. Bennett. They won 136 seats, routing Mackenzie King's Liberals who dropped to 89. The other seats were taken by the United Farmers of Alberta with nine, the Progressives with three, the Liberal Progressives with three, and Labour's two. McRae's strategy had worked well across the country. However, it faltered in B.C. where the Tories lost five seats. They took seven, the Liberals got five, and both the Labour and Independent parties each took one seat. There was tremendous irony in the result, however, because the man who plotted the campaign and was the architect of victory had gone down to personal defeat. As many had feared, the general lost by about 1,000 votes in the straight fight with Munn.

Author Arthur Ford wrote that McRae "more than any other man was responsible for the victory in 1930, an organizing genius who put all his talents and his untiring energy into that campaign." McRae had won in 1926 and sat for one term as an opposition member. Now four years later he had steered his party to power—it was in and he was out. He had known well the odds, and had also known that his vision was better when applied to the big picture. Perhaps it was all a noble sacrifice?

Bennett Distances Himself from McRae

Prime Minister R.B. Bennett's appreciation of the role McRae played in the Conservative leadership campaign and the 1930 election lasted about as long as politician's promises usually do. Almost immediately observers on Parliament Hill noted a distance developing between the two men. Although the general's approach to elected politics had always seemed ambivalent, his personal defeat in North Vancouver must have wounded him even if he had read the signs correctly and was prepared to sacrifice his own seat for the good of the party across the country.

His youngest daughter Peggy came from her home in New York to be with him on election night and shared with him the disappointing taste of his personal defeat. McRae's lack of public comment, with the absence of any written observations to describe his personal feelings, accentuate his stoicism, his dismissal of emotion as weakness, and his preference to be the private man when the opportunity afforded itself. Still, the irony of the election must have gnawed at him. Although the party he worked so hard to elect had won and now wielded the power, he wouldn't be there and had no chance to bring into being the policies he espoused.

McRae would have been a great asset in a Bennett government, and in the run-up to voting day some had touted him as a candidate for a senior cabinet post. His organizational skills, his business acumen and experience, and his personal relationships with financiers across Canada, the United States, and Britain would have been invaluable to the cabinet of a new government.

172

Bennett took over power when the worsening of the Great Depression rocked the world economy. He needed tough, talented, unflinching ministers for the hard days ahead, and McRae would have been perfect. There were two obvious moves Bennett could have made. He could have talked a winning Tory in a safe seat into giving it up and then parachuted McRae in for a by-election, or he could have appointed McRae to the Senate and immediately called him into the cabinet. He did neither. Bennett did create one by-election but it was for a veteran B.C. Tory, Vancouver's H.H. Stevens, who had also gone down to defeat after sitting in Parliament since 1911. He had held cabinet posts in previous Tory governments, and at age 52 was four years younger than McRae.

While Bennett pondered cabinet positions, the public read stories suggesting McRae was not in good health. This was contrary to the facts. He had long ago recovered from his fall on the ice and had worked tirelessly throughout the election campaign. There were predictions that McRae could be headed for the high commissioner's job in London, or the ambassador's post in Washington. The signs were out, however, when a small item appeared in Vancouver papers stating that Stevens had been called to Ottawa. When Bennett announced his cabinet in August, Stevens was named to the trade and commerce ministry and there was no mention of McRae. The prime minister stated that a by-election would be created in the East Kootenay riding, but it wasn't necessary to call out the voters because Stevens won by acclamation when no other candidates came forward.

Cabinets were much smaller in this nine-province era, and Bennett's first had sixteen ministers, including him. Ontario and Quebec took the bulk of the portfolios with the other provinces getting one each. Bennett, a Calgarian, represented Alberta and Stevens was B.C.'s man.

In September, Bennett also announced the resignation of Vincent Massey, the Liberal-appointed Canadian representative in London. An exchange of letters made it clear that he and the prime minister disagreed on the role of the high commissioner. The government wished to have a man with closer links to the administration in Ottawa. McRae, the ideal candidate, didn't get it. The prime minister had a great deal of both pride and vanity, and was a typically wary politician. He had tucked away in his mind the huge ovation given McRae at the 1927 convention, and the many stories that had touted him as a future leader. It was said Bennett had convinced himself the victory was his alone, although he was prepared to share some of the credit for the triumph with William H. Herridge, a senior member of his staff and a close confidant. Herridge had played a major role on the winning team and had the added advantage of being Bennett's brother-in-law, married to his much-beloved sister Mildred. Herridge later was made ambassador to the United States, another post many thought would have been better filled by McRae. Exactly what transpired between Bennett and McRae never became public knowledge. It seems certain, however, that there was a split and it was more than a minor one.

Finally in 1931 McRae accepted Bennett's offer of a Senate appointment. Again there are no papers or statements to give any indication why the general made the move, and why he decided—in effect—to paddle off into the backwater of the Canadian political scene rather than stand again for re-election. Had he finally convinced himself that he was, as journalist and Ottawa insider Gratton O'Leary wrote just before voting day, "better suited to political organization, his proven forte, than he was to political statesmanship?"

The Depression's Toll

Mackenzie King had refused to address the unemployment problem even when the Depression wrought havoc across the country and breadlines snaked through Vancouver and other cities. Thousands of ragged, starving people roamed the land desperately seeking work and assistance. There was little of either. The Liberal prime minister stubbornly maintained that most idle people had created their own problems—that there was a job for anyone who wanted one. There wasn't. He refused to allocate special funds for relief to meet the growing tragedy.

R.B. Bennett held to the same views as King, espousing the sanctity of the dollar and a balanced budget. He initially echoed the opinion that relief was the responsibility of the municipalities. Many cities like Vancouver swarmed with new arrivals searching hopelessly for work. When these money-starved municipalities went to the provinces, they, in turn, went to Ottawa, where they were turned down. The three levels of government passed the ball back and forth but always managed to drop it. Some still contended that handing out money would sap moral fibre, lead to sloth and laziness, and that many of those seeking help did not deserve a nickel. Meanwhile children sickened and died from malnutrition, tuberculosis, infectious diseases, and squalid housing conditions. Heartsick parents could do little to help, and city slums deteriorated as repair money dried up.

In 1932 Blanche Baker was elected president of the Junior League in Vancouver. The organization of wealthy young women enjoyed the social affairs sponsored by the club. Their lives in

Shaughnessy kept them far removed from the poverty and sickness on the other side of town. They did, however, pride themselves on being well informed about the woes of the world and had consistently made serious attempts to raise funds for needy causes such as hospitals and the Canadian National Institute for the Blind. With the Depression raging, the Junior League decided it should do something more to help young destitute mothers who could not afford the services of a doctor. They funded and staffed a well baby clinic for young mothers of their own age who often needed help in caring for their sick babies. As a money-making proposition Blanche introduced the idea of a thrift shop where used clothes and other items could be sold with the proceeds from the shop going to support the baby clinic. Every member donated clothes from her own cupboard. In its first year of operation the shop cleared $4,000, and it has been operating successfully ever since.

Blanche's tenure as president also saw the introduction of the Junior League's first newsletter as an attempt to keep the membership informed of their new project and to enlist more help in making the thrift shop a success. The newsletter just might have been a suggestion from her father, who was an acknowledged expert in this field because of his experience with the introduction of the ministry of information in Great Britain.

While many suffered during the Depression in a way that today is unimaginable, those who held a job lived through the misery relatively unscathed. A family could survive on an income of $40 a month or even less because in 1933 milk was a dime a quart, hamburger was eight cents a pound, bread was six cents a loaf, and a dozen eggs cost a quarter of a dollar. But for many who had run through their savings, sold their possessions, and didn't have any income, the prices were still too high.

Circumstances finally forced Bennett to provide relief money, but there were those who wouldn't take it out of pride until desperation forced them to accept the humiliating conditions under which it was dispensed. Some families received only three dollars a week. Those in need paid a heavy price for the government's refusal to recognize the problem or prepare for it.

Work camps set up by Ottawa sometimes produced harsher conditions than those in jail. All levels of government not only permitted but also relied on police brutality to beat back complainers; there were numerous deaths in the resulting violence and riots.

None suffered more than some of the people who had bought land on the prairies from McRae and Davidson. Barely 30 years old, the province of Saskatchewan was flat broke. Not only did the export markets for wheat collapse, but Saskatchewan and most of the prairies were hit by drought that dried up the land so much that nothing could grow. Howling winds scattered the topsoil and turned the waving luscious grass into a giant dustbowl. Cattle died and farms were repossessed. Some couldn't even grow food to feed themselves. It took several years for the land to recover and support the crops of the past. The survivors never forgot.

Officialdom might have been short on humanity, but the people of the country were not. There were many Canadians who shared what little they had. Dried fish was shipped to the desperate prairies by residents in Atlantic Canada. Church groups and other charity organizations shipped hampers and clothing to children who sometimes had nothing to wear but what could be made from old feed sacks. It was a time for compassion and courage, which could be found—along with the misery—across the country. Today a few old-timers still remember the fish and the hand-me-downs that made their lives bearable.

While there was no suffering at Hycroft, they weren't uncaring or unfeeling, and many like Blanche did something to help. Nonetheless there still lingered a belief that despite all the evidence some weren't doing all they could to help themselves. The papers were slow to plumb the depths of misery. For the public at large it didn't make much difference whether R.B. Bennett or Mackenzie King ran things; neither had the answers. Badly wounded by his defeat at the polls in 1930, the wily King eventually confided to his diary that it wasn't all that bad the Tories had to deal with the disaster as it grew worse. Late changes in policy by Bennett and the Tories failed to make a difference. Their failures paved the way for the Liberal's King to make a comeback.

McRae's Later Years

The Senate in the 1930s was held in higher esteem by the public as an unelected body than it was in the years to follow, but not by much. Toronto's *The Globe* commented that McRae got the appointment because he was an excellent party bagman and raiser of funds. It also predicted that the nature of the Senate could change because of him: "He will at all events add to its growing reputation as the abode of lively 'go-getters' who seem to sense sources from which party funds may be charmed." The Canadian Senate hasn't changed all that much in more than 130 years and why the newspaper thought that McRae could change its nature is difficult to discern.

With what was essentially a part-time job in Ottawa, McRae turned his attention to new opportunities in mining, oil exploration, and the development in the north. He became involved with the Texas-Canada Oil Company and the Pioneer Gold Mine in B.C.

He travelled the world, and then late in the decade—perhaps because of his new interest in northern development—took a long airplane trip, one of the most extensive ever made up to this time, through the Canadian north and Alaska. He took his youngest daughter Peggy along for company because he knew she needed a diversion. She and her husband Walter had been happily married for a number of years, but the Seligman family wanted an heir and she couldn't provide them with one. She was feeling the pressure from the family who wanted Walter to

During the early years of their marriage Walter and Peggy Seligman were members of the Havana Yacht Club, and spent a season each year in Cuba.

divorce her and marry someone who could give him children. So, when McRae planned his trip to the north he asked Peggy to come along, as it would give her a chance to talk about the situation if she wanted. Also, he had always enjoyed her company and her high spirits. Peggy, like her father, had become a globetrotter, and had kept a scrapbook of pictures from her travels to Havana, Jamaica, Hungary, Paris, and many other parts of the world. During a trip to Hungary she was pictured in the colourful local dress. On their trip to the north together they visited isolated, almost unknown settlements, in areas that had been seen by only the most adventurous. McRae began what soon became an extensive library of books and papers on Alaska and the Canadian north as well as a collection of Eskimo art. The extensive adventure by air was one of the most far-reaching taken by any MP or senator, or indeed any Canadian, up to that time. It was also the beginning of a new era for McRae as he became something of an expert on the Canadian north and Alaska.

As he approached his 60th birthday McRae spent more of his leisure time at Hycroft, where he had always maintained a keen interest in the gardens, the shrubbery, and trees that made the estate a showplace. Although Hycroft remained one of Vancouver's top social centres, the hectic and carefree pace of the 1920s was supplanted by the more subdued 1930s. The McRaes were now older, and so were many of their guests.

Senator McRae dutifully attended to his Ottawa duties. On March 15, 1933 he made some rueful comments during a debate on the question of election expenses. It was suggested they be held down to $4,000 per riding, and McRae told the house "it cost me several times $4,000 to be a defeated candidate in the last election." He also said that the modern airplane and improvements in other transportation in Canada meant that a much shorter time for election campaigns was required, and suggested three weeks was enough. His proposal was ignored; even in 2000 the campaign was still five weeks. McRae also told the Senate that he favoured the Australian system of compulsory voting.

In the chamber on February 1, 1934 McRae predicted with chilling accuracy that another war in Europe would erupt within five years. He was only about six months out. German guns started to roar in Poland in September 1939, and a new wave of global slaughter began that would take 50,000 Canadian lives before it was over. He told his Senate colleagues that he had met some 25 prominent men at various meetings in France, Germany, and Austria. He didn't give names or indicate their positions but said, "Invariably I asked them whether I was right in believing that racial ambitions, hatreds and struggles were more rampant in Europe today than they were twenty years ago and invariably I received the answer that I was correct. As I see it Europe is rapidly becoming an armed camp. There is more talk of war in Europe today than there was in the early part of 1914. In my judgment European war is a certainty and will occur within five years."

McRae also reaffirmed his earlier beliefs that the League of Nations had failed to establish peace in the world. He said Hitler, who had come to power a few years earlier, was laying a strong foundation for his regime. Turning again to his prediction of war, McRae stated: "I can not conceive of any developments which would justify sacrificing the blood of one single Canadian in the battlefields of Europe." The records of the Senate debates note

As McRae grew older and had more time to spend at home, he happily chatted with his gardeners about the shrubs and flowers he wanted to feature at Hycroft for the next season.

shouts of "Hear, hear!" to McRae's condemnation of the League of Nations.

In his wide-ranging speech that day, the senator said Canada's main problems were unemployment, the high cost of government, and unsaleable wheat. He stated that on his recent European trip he had seen tariff walls getting higher and higher. He felt that Canada's best trade chances were tied to the Empire, although the British still had to be convinced that this approach would not interfere in their trade with countries outside the group. They stayed unconvinced.

McRae blamed governments for permitting some 30,000 farmers to establish farms in southwestern Saskatchewan and southeastern Alberta for growing grain on land that was better suited for ranching. He knew this area and its possibilities as well as its problems. The senator called for government aid for these destitute farmers and suggested one solution: blanket bankruptcy. While he remained opposed to a welfare-state concept, McRae believed that there was always a time and place for direct government aid to people when circumstances warranted it.

McRae, not a vengeful man, must have watched with very mixed feelings and appreciated the irony in the defeat of Bennett in the 1935 election. Bennett was a resolute man who did not back down easily from what he perceived to be the right course. However, he was battered by political opponents, the public, and the media for not solving the Depression's woes. He simply held the reins at the wrong time when his unswerving, conservative views were unable to meet new needs and challenges. He had worked tirelessly, was worn down, and his health was suffering. As the situation deteriorated and the attacks increased, Bennett also faced dissension with-

Colour was important to Blaunche, and when she entertained in the summer she often wore a blue dress to match the delphiniums in the garden.

in his party. The irony, as McRae readily appreciated, was that the most damaging blow came from Stevens, Bennett's B.C. choice for cabinet. Stevens broke from the Tories and formed a Reconstruction Party, which like McRae's short-lived Provincial Party in B.C., was slaughtered at the next election polls. Stevens was the only winning candidate. There was a striking parallel. The Reconstruction Party had helped split the vote in many ridings as had McRae's group in B.C. in 1924. The Liberals took 171 seats and the Conservatives a humbling 39, and it was calculated that but for the Reconstruction Party vote they would have held at least another 50 seats.

Bennett hung on as leader until 1938. While he obviously was on the way out, it was a further deterioration of his health that clinched his retirement. He was also distraught at the sudden death of his sister, Mildred Herridge, who had been a companion and frequent hostess for her bachelor brother. He surprised many friends by moving to England in 1939. He purchased a small estate in Surrey called Juniper Hill that had belonged to a fellow, former Canadian, Lord Beaverbrook, who had lobbied in McRae's interests in the First World War. Bennett was honoured with a peerage in 1941, which entitled him to sit in the House of Lords as a viscount. Continuing ill health restricted his political and social life, however, and he died at Juniper Hill a few days before his 77th birthday in 1947.

After Bennett retired, McRae's name came up once more as a potential leader of the Conservative Party as it was again in trouble and going nowhere. In May 1938 the *Canadian Magazine* stated that the 62-year-old senator could be a contender because he was a liberal-minded man "who cordially detests the sham and hypocrisy beloved by so many." While the magazine story speculated that he might appeal to younger Tories as well as older ones, this idea was no more than an improbable proposition dreamed up by the writer. For the rest of his life McRae didn't venture politically beyond the Senate chamber. The Conservatives chose R.J. Manion as their leader, who had a brief and unspectacular reign and was unable to overturn Mackenzie King.

In 1935, after several years of travel and a slightly more relaxed lifestyle, McRae decided to take on a new challenge as a gentleman rancher and farmer. Perhaps it was his genuine concern for the farmers of Alberta during the early 1930s or his happy memories of childhood on the farm in Glencoe that sparked his desire to return to the land; however, the farm he conceived encompassed a vision far larger and far more diversified than anyone else could have imagined. The resulting farming estate was the largest ever created on Vancouver Island. He called it Eaglecrest.

Eaglecrest—McRae's Last Dream

As the 1930s advanced McRae spent more time with his family. His entertaining at Hycroft was not as lavish as it had been because he felt the opulent, splendid balls of the past were inappropriate when so many were suffering from the poverty brought on by unemployment. In addition, he was no longer involved in political campaigning. The doors of the estate still swung open but the parties were smaller, and the McRaes now hosted children and grandchildren, as much as politicians and world leaders. The only really large affairs were fund-raising events for charity organizations.

Early in the decade while scouting land for his planned country estate, Alexander Duncan McRae found Qualicum Beach. As always his ideas and plans were on a scale seldom envisioned by others; soon his enthusiasm spread to all members of the family. McRae purchased 260 acres of land located off the eastern end of Qualicum Beach, running from the Island Highway north to the shoreline. Located on a bluff overlooking the sea, it was to be the site of a magnificent new country lodge he would call "Eaglecrest."

Among McRae's priorities for the property was land that would support the horses he, his wife, their daughters, and friends loved to ride. Vancouver had grown and it was difficult to find good riding trails in the city, so he often took his children and grandchildren to the Caribou country where they could ride the range and the rolling hills of the Flying U Ranch at 70 Mile House. One of his granddaughters later remarked, "I loved the Caribou even more than our holidays at Eaglecrest and I think that's why I decided later on to become a rancher." McRae's thoughts undoubtedly also harkened back to his early days on the farm in Glencoe for his ideas for his new estate at Eaglecrest went far beyond establishing a good stable of horses. He wanted to breed a variety of farm animals, to cultivate and improve crops, and to experiment with them. It was not long before he added an additional 4,000 acres to his holdings in the Qualicum area. These farming lands were located on the other side of the town in the shadow of Mount Arrowsmith and included meadows and forests as well as Hamilton Marsh, which he proceeded to drain so that the land could be cultivated.

Never satisfied with anything but the biggest and the best, McRae's ideas for Eaglecrest—what was essentially his "country" home—and the surrounding 260 acres of beachfront property were grander than anything seen before on central Vancouver Island. When he began construction of the lodge, the depths of the Depression had reached even this small community. Qualicum, like many other villages, was struggling to survive. McRae's arrival changed everything. For two years, beginning in 1934, 25 men were employed full-time on the construction of the sprawling log house and other nearby outbuildings the likes of which had never been seen before in the tiny community.

The main house, made of whole cedar logs, was 200 feet long and 50 feet across. The living room alone was 50 feet square with a ceiling that soared to 26 feet at its peak. To the right and left of this great room hallways led on one side to the dining room and kitchen and on the other side to self-contained suites of rooms for McRae and Blaunche. Above the suites was a dormitory that provided additional sleeping for up to twelve people. The house had a central heating system as well as four giant stone fireplaces, each of them six or seven feet in width.

The building that housed the servants was separate from the main house, providing privacy for both the family and for the three men and three women who served them and their guests.

McRae hired only local people, and the tradesmen and artisans of Qualicum repaid him by practising their crafts with pride and

Eaglecrest was a country estate that only McRae could have devised. A sprawling 200-foot long building made of whole logs was centred on the main lounge, which was 50 feet square and featured a huge fireplace and grand staircase.

The family soon spent much of their time at Eaglecrest and there was always room for guests who enjoyed swimming, fishing, or horseback riding. Pictured on the porch which overlooked Qualicum Bay are Lucile (left) and Peggy.

McRae developed a strong and lasting friendship with Peggy's husband, Walter Seligman, who was frequently a guest on trips to the north and at Eaglecrest. Here Walter chats with his in-laws during one of his many visits to Qualicum Beach.

joy. Nowhere else could they have obtained steady employment at good wages for a full two years with the added incentive of being provided with only the best available raw materials.

Some of the logs for the lodge and outbuildings, which included servants' quarters, a garage, and a stable, were cut on his property; others came from farther away, up in the hills. All of them were cut during one three-week period each year in the very short space of time between when the sap starts to flow and new growth begins. The sap must begin to flow so the logs can be peeled easily, but they must not be cut after growth begins or they will be subject to mould and will turn an ugly grey colour.

Vancouver Sun reporter Roy Brown wrote, "In Vancouver, Ottawa, or London, it might be 'Hello—Senator McRae,' but on Vancouver Island where he was a farmer it was plain A.D." Brown said McRae was a farmer citizen of Qualicum who turned to his neighbours for advice and the workforce he required to achieve his dream. All the contracts for clearing, construction, digging, and fence building went to Qualicum people; McRae also insisted that all materials be acquired locally. Brown added, "The first

The dormitory upstairs could sleep up to ten overnight guests.

homestead at Eaglecrest was of course a millionaires' plaything, but then he moved out towards the Alberni highway and his contractors carved the greatest single farm in the province out of the wilderness."

Torchy Anderson, a well-known *Vancouver Province* writer, described some of the construction he witnessed at Eaglecrest, "Even the bolts are being made on the job. A smith has been installed under the alders and is kept busy turning out his hand-forged material."

Water was pumped from several springs on the property for use in the house and outbuildings, and as the lodge was being constructed, grass covered bridle paths were laid out where the family could enjoy their favorite sport, horseback riding. Before his three granddaughters arrived for their first summer vacation at Eaglecrest, McRae had purchased a pony for each of them from the Flying U Ranch in the Caribou. There was also a grass bowling green and golf putting greens laid out near the house.

Torchy Anderson's colourful description of the view from the bluffs at Eaglecrest explains McRae's choice of the site for his country home: "As the ruffled waters of the Strait run from

Like Hycroft, Eaglecrest was soon covered with Virginia creeper. The long drive to the house led through woods, ending in a circular drive in front of the house.

The huge fireplace in the main lounge was nearly ten feet wide and built to burn the huge logs cut on the property or salvaged from the beach.

The years at Eaglecrest were more relaxed. Senator McRae enjoyed the role of gentleman farmer and Blaunche was content with the more informal entertaining that was possible there. McRae's study, adorned with stuffed wild animals, swords, and suits of armour, was also filled with hundreds of books, many of them collected during his travels in the north.

blue to leaden grey, to sunset crimson, and, almost before you know it, the path of a moon comes twinkling across the sea, you will understand why General McRae is going to Qualicum. Turn away from the sea and drive slowly through the woods where the arbutus stand, delicately aloof from towering firs and cedars, catch the sweet air that comes fresh from the snowcaps, scented by a thousand flowering shrubs and you will wonder if the general will ever want to live anywhere else."

The McRaes went to London in 1935, which was the same year that R.B. Bennett and the Tories went down to defeat in Ottawa at the hands of a resurgent Mackenzie King and his Liberals. McRae had little interest in the election; it would not really affect his duties as senator and he was now committed to new interests in the north and with the development of his property in Qualicum. While in Great Britain he visited Scotland where he bought 71 sheep and persuaded several shepherds and

Three generations of the McRae family gathered at Eaglecrest in 1943. Pictured left to right are Audrey Baker, Alexander and Blaunche McRae with Walter Seligman seated in front of them, Peggy Seligman, Jocelyn Baker, Lucile Paul, and Bebe Paul.

Even the card room, often used for other games as well as reading, contained an enormous fireplace.

their sheep dogs to come with the herd to Vancouver Island. He also found shorthorn cattle of a size and breeding that appealed to him and bought eight head for shipment across the ocean to Vancouver Island. He sought the best horses, the best dairy cattle, and the best pigs he could find and transported them all to his growing estate. There were even ducks for the ponds and special runs for geese. A visitor once commented the pigpens were so clean you could almost eat off the floor.

The farm became a paradise for livestock and the best place in the country for farmhands to work. Together McRae and his men experimented with improving breeds and providing better feed for the animals, and achieved some measure of success. The centre of these activities was one of the largest barns ever built on the island or anywhere else up to that time. It was 204 feet long with an average width of 80 feet, which expanded at the middle to 204 feet. While McRae owned the farm—a period of thirteen to fourteen years—he employed 100 men on a full-time basis to feed and care for his animals. Eight miles of six-foot high fencing encircled the whole area.

Blaunche had enthusiastically become involved in the Eaglecrest project, laying out the network of bridal paths and supervising the interior finishing of the house. Much of Eaglecrest was furnished with Canadian-made cabinetry from Quebec, each piece carefully chosen by Blaunche. The remainder was French provincial or favourite antiques shipped from Hycroft, some acquired over the years in Europe. She also purchased three Cadillacs for use on the property, and later, a LaSalle convertible used to transport visiting grandchildren and their friends around the neighbourhood.

Eaglecrest was a delightful place for each of the granddaughters to visit. The youngest, Audrey (Baker) Wittner, recalls that as a child of about twelve her grandfather gave her a job weeding one of the long flowerbeds. "I was very proud of my 50 cents an hour," she said. McRae may have decided on the rate of pay after recalling that he had worked for his father in Glencoe for 50 cents a day.

He also allowed Audrey to train and show one of his shorthorn heifers at the Pacific National Exhibition. "Imagine my delight when we captured reserve champion," she commented. The reward was, however, tempered with some annoyance when the heifer smashed the young girl's nose against a stall on the way back to the barn.

Both Jocelyn (Baker) Roche and Audrey (Baker) Wittner recalled sleeping in the dormitory at Eaglecrest. The whole Qualicum estate was a delight for these two and their cousin Bebe Paul, but sleeping in the loft had its drawbacks. It was only accessible through the living room, so there was no way to sneak in or out once they were sent to bed. "We used to sneak down to get chocolates which were always around because guests brought them as gifts for grandmother," explained Jocelyn. "The governess had to be sure we didn't eat too many."

Both girls gained lifelong friends from their days at Eaglecrest. For Jocelyn it was the governess, Betty Simpson (later McMurphy), who was only a couple of years older than her. The two women visited each other frequently until McMurphy's death in 1998. For Audrey it was the groom's daughter Jackie, whom she first met at Hycroft. "When Eaglecrest was built Jackie's family moved to Qualicum," she explained, "And when I was visiting we seldom saw the adults as we were always at the beach or riding, or Jackie and I were off in the woods building forts … We always had the most wonderful time at Eaglecrest."

Audrey remembers that her grandfather had a wonderful smile and that he was a terrible tease. He had very strong likes and dislikes and hated the word "cute" when it was used to describe a person. He said no male over the age of two could be considered "cute." McRae often talked to his grandchildren and their friends who visited in the summer, and one remembers him saying to her, "Deciding who you are going to marry is the most important decision you will make in your life. Don't be too hasty about it."

Blaunche McRae's love of horses and dogs was evident throughout her life, but as she grew older, the size of her dogs diminished. At Hycroft the dogs had been huge Bull Mastiffs or Great Danes; at Eaglecrest they were Pekingese. One old family friend said that at one time she thought there were at least six at the Qualicum estate.

The Final Act

Vancouver's 50th birthday was held in 1936, and the golden jubilee was marked back at Hycroft on McRae Avenue at a series of special functions. The first names in the guest book for a reception were those of Sir Percy Vincent, the Lord Mayor of London, and Lady Vincent. As guests departed in 1936, McRae and his wife hurried back to the Island to entertain formally for the first time at Eaglecrest; their visitor, an old family friend, was former Lieutenant Governor John Nichol.

The guest book at Hycroft contained the names of princes and presidents, millionaires, dukes, and duchesses. The names appeared along with all the other high-ranking visitors from Britain and Ottawa and around the world who attended festivities over the years at the palatial home. Among the best known were the Prince of Wales, the Duke of Kent, and the Duke and Duchess of Connaught.

They had given him a standing ovation in Winnipeg eleven years earlier—reportedly a half-hour's cheering according to the *Province's* account of it—and so the Conservative Party decided belatedly to honour Senator McRae in a more tangible way. It took them until July 6, 1938 to get around to it, and why there was such a long delay isn't quite clear, although McRae's friends in the party might have waited until Bennett was gone. In a brief ceremony McRae received a handsome grandfather clock in recognition of his superb organization of the 1927 leadership convention. He had, of course, been the architect of the winning campaign in 1930 that put Bennett and the party into government in Ottawa, but it was not mentioned. The handsome clock was shipped to Eaglecrest.

McRae was once again a very busy man, dividing his time between Parliament, his farm, and Hycroft. There was still much activity at the mansion, and the papers reported it faithfully. One social reporter described Blaunche McRae as "quiet, sensible, a great hostess and a good horsewoman." In the spring of 1938 she opened the house and its grounds for an Imperial Order, Daughters of the Empire (IODE) garden fete. Her "At Home" at Hycroft on August 4 that year was held on a "most glorious day," with readers learning that Mrs. McRae was "smartly gowned in delphinium blue chiffon. The grass-length dress was worn with a short jacket of the same material and colour." Blaunche McRae was also named a judge of the junior and senior saddle classes at the horse show during Exhibition Week, a tribute to her long experience with horses and riding.

It was about this time that McRae commissioned a well-known Vancouver photographer to take pictures of Hycroft, showing the mansion at its best. He seems to have known the world was changing and wanted to remember their house as it was that summer. The photographer was Leonard Frank; he took photos on several occasions from many angles. McRae was pleased with many of the photos, but did not like the bill he received and wrote to Frank about it. The letter states: "My Dear Leonard, I have sufficiently recovered from your stupendous bill to be able to write to you. It looks to me very, very excessive. I am enclosing a cheque for $500 which I trust you will consider a payment of the account in full." It is signed, "Kindest regards, McRae." It is not known whether Leonard Frank accepted the $500 payment or continued to hound McRae for additional payments.

That same summer McRae made an extended trip to visit his properties in the north, taking with him his daughter Blanche, his granddaughter Jocelyn, and son-in-law Walter Seligman, who had become one of the senator's close friends. Jocelyn recalls sharing a tent with her mother while her grandfather and Uncle Walter shared the other one. They visited two mines in Alaska, one in the Yukon, and two near Atlin in B.C.

McRae, Blanche, and his granddaughter Jocelyn made an extended tour of northern B.C., the Yukon, and Alaska in 1941. Walter Seligman was also along for the trip to inspect some of the mining operations McRae had purchased there.

For the McRaes life was fulfilling and even peaceful at times, but the mood was not to last. One year later, in September 1939, Canada was again plunged into war in Europe. McRae had predicted it and had earned no friends with his argument that Canada should do all it could to not be involved in another blood bath. The carnage that took some 60,000 Canadian lives had been over little more than twenty years when McRae criticized Canada's state of preparedness for the new conflict, which was to kill 50,000 more. The armed forces had been run down since the end of the First World War, and Canadian industry was not geared to meet the needs of war.

McRae's sharp criticism might possibly be attributed to the fact that he was not called on to play a role as Canada mobilized its strength for the conflict. After all, his record in the First World War was impeccable, and he had been recognized for his abilities and his efforts. He was still a young thinker, a modern man with ideas and innovations—not a relic living in the glories of the past. But his involvement this time was limited to being head of the Canadian War Services campaign. He pulled together fund-raising for such organizations as the Canadian Legion and the Young Men's Christian Association (YMCA) to provide non-military support and care for service men and their families. When McRae took over he quickly pointed out that in the interests of achieving maximum results it was nonsense to have several campaigns for money instead of one. At the age of 65 he did the job well, but it would seem that he could have contributed much more to the war effort if he had been asked.

The three McRae daughters—Blanche, Lucile, and Peggy—organized one last giant ball at Hycroft on the eve of 1942. Their mother had been ill for some time when the request came from the Red Cross to hold the fund-raising event at Hycroft, so the girls took on the task of decorating the house and hiring the caterers while members of the Red Cross sold tickets to the event. It was far different from the balls of old, but still a grand affair. It was open to the public; in fact, to anyone who wanted to purchase a ticket and was prepared to dress for the occasion, although fire regulations limited the number permitted to attend.

There were men and women in uniform instead of fancy dress at this final New Year's Eve ball. McRae's granddaughter Jocelyn Baker, Blanche's daughter, had her "coming-out" as a debutant at the ball. Because of the war there were only four debutantes honoured that year at Hycroft: Jocelyn, her cousin Rosemary Baker, Barbara Golding, and Nancy Fleck. The *Vancouver Sun* ran a picture of Jocelyn, announcing that Miss Jocelyn Baker, a granddaughter of Senator and Mrs. McRae was seen dancing with Judson Armstrong of the RCAF. Mrs. McRae, Mistress of Hycroft, elegantly dressed but looking tired was pictured smiling, seated in an easy chair in the foyer. It was far different from the masquerade balls of years gone by, and none of those who appeared in a newspaper picture snake-dancing through Hycroft's ballroom and bar knew it was the last time there would be such an event hosted by the McRaes. No one knew that the curtain was coming down on the final act. The McRaes left the next day to spend the winter in Arizona.

By the winter of 1941-42 Hycroft had actually been vacant for a number of months; Alexander and Blaunche were living in the Vancouver Hotel. She had not been well for several months, and there were problems getting fuel to heat the huge house. It was too big to manage without help, and there was no help to be found because all the young men and women had enlisted in the armed services as soon as they came of age or worked in factories supplying the needs of war. A year later, in 1943, a severe winter and a lack of fuel brought the closure of all high schools for six weeks because there was no way to heat them.

Soon after the final ball McRae's two granddaughters, Jocelyn and Audrey Baker, enlisted in the armed services, Jocelyn in the navy and Audrey in the army.

Late in 1942 the McRaes announced that they were giving the home they had built and lived in for almost 30 years to the federal government for use as a military hospital. It was their very significant contribution to the war effort. The house was officially "sold" to Ottawa for one dollar, undoubtedly one of the better financial deals the government had ever made. McRae often was described as a philanthropist, but there are no records to trace donations other than the very generous gift of Hycroft. Still subject to the criticism of the media, McRae's generosity was questioned by the *Vancouver News Herald*, which asked if this was McRae's way of getting rid of what the newspaper said had been called a "white elephant." It stated that Hycroft had been assessed at $150,000 in 1942 and that annual taxes were about $5,000. The paper asked if there was much tax money owing on the house that the city or the federal government would be stuck with? It was a petty, mean argument as McRae was a very rich man and hardly likely to welch on a few thousand in taxes. A brief statement was issued by a city hall official, stating that there was nothing owing on Hycroft.

The McRaes returned from Arizona to spend the summer at Eaglecrest, and then moved again to the Vancouver Hotel for the winter. It was there on November 10, 1942 that Blaunche Latimer McRae died of cancer. Her funeral was held in the home she had created and enjoyed for 30 years. This, the final function for the McRae family at Hycroft, took place on November 13, 1942 at 2:30 p.m. The *Vancouver Province* reported, "In the autumn-toned setting of the famous gardens and stately halls of Hycroft last rites were held for Mrs. Blaunche McRae, wife of General A. D. McRae, senator, on Friday afternoon. Mrs. McRae died Tuesday after a long illness … she became known as one of the city's social leaders and outstanding hostesses." Reverend Harrison Villett read the service, and interment took place at the Abbey, Ocean View. The pallbearers included Major Austin Taylor, Percival McKergow, Colonel H. S. Tobin, Percival Kirkpatrick, W. F. Tucker Battle, and D. G. Marshall.

The funeral was a fitting conclusion to the McRaes' years at Hycroft. Blaunche would never again set foot in the home she had created, nor would anyone else see it the way it had once been. Her death brought an end to it all.

In the weeks before the furnishings were auctioned off, McRae often walked the streets of the South Granville area, perhaps just to be out in the neighbourhood that had been home for so long. Hycroft was not a place to live alone. In those days Purdy's Chocolates had a store in the vicinity, and the girls at the counter recalled talking to him several times. One said, "I think it was a very lonely time for him."

Hycroft Under the Hammer

Charles Dawson, Vancouver Auctioneer and Appraiser, gave this report.

I have been in the auctioneering business in Vancouver for many years, but even I felt the excitement when I was asked to conduct the auction sale at Hycroft after the McRaes gave it to the federal government for a hospital. This was more than just a sale at a big house; this was the dissolution of a mansion, the end of an era that began in Vancouver's glory days. For some who came for the sale and to buy a small item as a souvenir, there were memories in all those gracious rooms and in the sweep of the staircase with the stain-glassed window behind it. It was easy to recall again the laughter, the music, the sparkling glasses in the bar, the sounds of dancing feet, and the happy cries of children looking at the huge tree ablaze with lights and the glittering decorations of Christmas. From the beginning Hycroft had epitomized elegance and style, and life was lived there accordingly. It was the mecca of the city's social set through good times and bad, economic booms and depressions, a world war that claimed the lives of many of the young men who had danced in its ballroom and romanced girls in its gardens. Now in 1942 it was to start serving a grimmer purpose. During the Depression in the '30s I sold the possessions of quite a few of the grander homes in Shaughnessy when the owners fortunes fell as the market crashed and hard times hit "Mortgage Heights" but nothing compared to Hycroft's sale.

Mrs. McRae had been an eclectic collector of all kinds of furnishings and had bought her possessions around the world. The Senator liked his elegant, comfortable surroundings, but the interior of Hycroft was basically her doing. She had exquisite taste and loved opulence. Some of her treasures had been purchased from the estate of Ludwig the Second of Bavaria. When it was fully laid for a banquet, the McRae's long, mahogany dining room table, with its fourteen matching chairs, fine crystal, china, and gleaming solid, antique silverware, reflected the elegance of the Victorian-Edwardian eras like nothing else in Vancouver. Seeing it you could imagine the finest foods prepared to perfection and vintage wines served by white-gloved waiters. On the dining room floor was a twenty- by sixteen-foot imported rug in green and fawn with a floral border, one of the best I had ever seen.

The war news was not good in the winter of 1942 and people had more on their minds than auction sales. I'm sure there would have been even more interest in the dissolution of the house if times had been different. Viewing was on Saturday, December 12 and there was a good crowd of prospective buyers and the simply curious who had never had the chance to see the inside of the house before. Because of the time of year it was fairly easy to imagine how the house and gardens had looked in their pre-Christmas finery and the decorations in the ballroom for the famous McRae New Year's Eve fancy-dress balls.

Admission to the sale when it opened on Monday was by purchase of a 30-cent catalogue. There was a good crowd and bidding was brisk but probably because of the times, prices were not what they might have been. Astute buyers of the finer things got some great bargains. Quite a few items were withdrawn from sale because the reserved price wasn't reached in the bidding. Mrs. McRae also had taken some of her favourite pieces to their estate at Eaglecrest on Vancouver Island, but still listed was a treasure trove, much of it of English origin. Surprisingly there were no paintings of any great distinction, but there were many other very tasteful and expensive objects d'art.

The dining-room was particularly lavish. There was delicate china from Royal Doulton, Moorcroft, Coalport, Royal Crown Derby, Wedgwood, Minton, and from many European manufacturers. There were hundreds of crystal glasses of all styles, including the best of Bohemian glassware from Czechoslovakia. There were place settings in silver, with boullion spoons, fish knives and forks, oyster forks, silver serving bowls, plates and comports, game-carving scissors, silver salt and peppers, a silver tea caddy, and silver ashtrays. There were few suggested prices in the catalogue, but there was a spectacular antique six-piece tea and coffee set which I had appraised for at least $1,000. Table decorations included three large Dutch-made silver pheasants with moveable wings.

There were carpets from England, India, China, Persia, Turkey and Baluchistan; tapestries from France and Belgium, and paintings by several European artists, although as I stated, none of them were by leading artists. Also for sale were Chinese tomb horses from the Tang dynasty, 617-906 A.D., and bronze statuary from Italy along with Sevres urns and stained glass.

Throughout the house there were solid tables, sideboards, chairs and footstools in the Elizabethan, Jacobean and other styles. The library had a floor-to-ceiling collection of old, often leather-bound books. There was a 1611 collection of bibles. A large number of books had already been donated by Mrs. McRae to the Imperial Order, Daughters of the Empire (IODE). The Senator also had not chosen, or perhaps overlooked, taking his histories of the Clan McRae and the 6th Battalion of the Canadian-Scottish Regiment 1914-18.

If your taste ran to that sort of thing there was a very large, mounted buffalo head. One of the most popular items was the more than 100 small mirrors from the wall of the downstairs bar. That was a pretty good keep-sake for a whole lot of people.

The master bedroom contained a striking eight-piece English mahogany suite, an Italian marble bust, a silver ink stand, a chaise lounge, and silk curtains. The other bedrooms were similarly comfortably and well appointed. There was an English enamelled bed with painted decorations, several Axminister rugs, and a set of boudoir lamps with silk shades. Throughout the house there were also candlesticks in brass, crystal and silver. Everything was for sale including the statuary in the gardens, works in ceramic and brass, and sculptures in marble.

It was a long sale but still many people witnessed it all. I'm not at liberty to disclose how much money was realized as this was a private matter for the McRaes. There was a newspaper report which stated the total was about $50,000, according to someone who contended he sat through the entire sale and counted it up. I can only comment that this figure tends to the low side. To repeat myself, at another time I'm sure the bidding would have gone considerably higher. It was, however, the most spectacular auction sale I have ever presided over, and I have conducted a good many. The wide range of goods is unlikely to be repeated in Vancouver because Hycroft, after all, was unique. In many ways it was sad to see the end of an era and a style which is also gone. There were those who went home happy with their small purchases, souvenirs of exciting, glamorous nights when they had been among the thousands whom the McRaes had entertained in the heyday of the mansion on the hill.

Hycroft Hospital

Before the auction McRae's daughters visited their former home and took mementos—things they had treasured most—from the house, and McRae moved his most prized possessions to Eaglecrest, but everything else was sold. Not one of them attended the final demise of the home that they had lived in and loved for so long, where they had played, and where their children had played. Two generations had gone exploring in the intriguing old mansion and finalized in the Italian garden and playhouse.

The military immediately converted Hycroft into a 125-bed annex for Shaughnessy Military Hospital. It was used primarily for older First World War veterans who still needed medical care, thereby taking pressure off the main hospital that handled casualties from the current war.

McRae Avenue and the surrounding streets were packed with cars when some 3,000 people turned up on August 9, 1943 for the official opening of the hospital. It was a moving and sentimental experience for McRae. In the century's first decade he had bought a bare Shaughnessy hillside, built his mansion, planted his sequoia, nurtured his gardens, raised his family, hosted many people and events, and experienced the wins and defeats that fate had dealt him in life, all the while watching—from the front terrace of his home—the city of Vancouver growing up around him.

Standing in the glorious gardens with the flowers, shrubs, and trees in full bloom and never looking better, McRae, now a widower nearing 70, told the huge crowd that Hycroft had been a happy home. Looking at it with fond memories, he knew full well that times were changing, and he acknowledged the fact. "There will be fewer structures of this kind in Canada in the future," said the senator. The man who had made millions as an entrepreneur in a time when Canada had no income tax added, "With more equal distribution of wealth and taxes, those more fortunate will have to share with others." He wasn't complaining, just stating the obvious. The crowd gave him a generous round of applause. An old political opponent, federal Minister of Pensions and National Health Ian McKenzie, thanked McRae and his late wife, the chatelaine, for this gift to Canada. He added that without any doubt Hycroft would become the "most exquisite hospital annex" in all North America, a beautiful place to be enjoyed in comfort by those who deserved it by their service to their country. Until he died, McRae would return often to Hycroft to chat with the veterans and revisit his former "happy home."

To McRae's three daughters the loss of Hycroft was traumatic. One of them was moved to comment, "And so our beloved Hycroft which I first saw when I was just a child in 1911, where I grew up, and danced the nights away has faded into history for us. It has begun a very different life, a place where the sick and dying are treated with compassion and where they can find some peace as they stroll in the gardens or watch the seasons come and go from their hospital beds. It is not a bad end, I guess."

About a year after his first wife died, McRae remarried. Like Blaunche, his second wife, Mrs. Louise Rhodes, was an American, but from El Paso, Texas. Mrs. Rhodes, 50, had been a widow for about fifteen years. Alexander and Louise were married on October 10, 1943, in the Presbyterian Church on Fifth Avenue in New York City. When she was not travelling with her husband, the new Mrs. McRae spent the remainder of the short time they were married at Eaglecrest.

McRae's second marriage in 1943 was followed by another family wedding in 1944. McRae's oldest daughter Blanche divorced her first husband Richard Baker and remarried, becoming Mrs. Daniel Beynon Lewis on September 30, 1944. The wedding took place in the chapel at Canadian Memorial United Church with just the family in attendance. General McRae

As Peggy's marriage to Walter came to an end she spent a quiet summer at Qualicum Beach. She did not stay quiet for long.

gave the bride away and Reverend Harrison Villett performed the ceremony. Leading Wren, Jocelyn Baker, was her mother's only attendant. Audrey was stationed in Ottawa at the time and did not make the trip home, but the bride's two sisters, Lucile and Peggy, were both on hand. Newspapers said the couple would reside at 1664 Cedar Crescent, only a block or two from McRae Avenue, but it was not to be for long.

Within weeks Blanche was diagnosed with tuberculosis and entered the Tranquille sanatorium near Kamloops. That same year Jocelyn was invalided out of the Wrens and into a hospital in Victoria with an injured back. Although she would be plagued throughout her life with back problems, she recovered well enough to leave the hospital and go to Eaglecrest to spend some time with her grandfather. Blanche was still in Tranquille; but McRae, always supportive of his family, soon arranged to have her transferred to Victoria so that he and Jocelyn would be able to visit her on a more regular basis.

Jocelyn recalls that the chauffeur drove the two of them from Eaglecrest to Victoria just a week before her mother died from the debilitating disease that had wracked her body. Blanche's

205

new marriage lasted less than a year. Her funeral was held on September 4, 1945 in Canadian Memorial where she had been married only months earlier. The same Reverend Villett conducted the service at noon, and Blanche's body was interred near her mother in the Abbey at Ocean View cemetery. Newspapers said she left to mourn her new husband Daniel Lewis, her father Alexander Duncan McRae, her two sisters, and her two daughters.

Shortly after her sister's death, Peggy's marriage to Walter Seligman ended. He divorced her because of pressure from his family to produce an heir for the Seligman fortune. Peggy had known it was coming; in fact, she had had her

Peggy's second marriage to Bruce Hay Chapman of Santa Barbara brought with it two step-children and a new life in California.

own plans. During the summer of 1945 she introduced her father to Bruce Hay Chapman of Santa Barbara, California who became her husband on March 20, 1946. Her father attended the ceremony in Santa Barbara where he met Peggy's two step-children: Anita Bruce Chapman, who at the time was nine, and William Spencer Chapman, who was just three years old.

One other marriage took place about this time. Lucile's only daughter Blanche Beverly Paul, born in 1925 and nicknamed "Bebe," married Arthur E. Placker in Fort Lewis, Washington on June 18, 1944. Bebe had two daughters: Lucile, born in 1950, and Maureen, born in 1955. She later remarried and moved first to Oklahoma and finally to Arkansas where she died.

A Titan Falls

Time passed quickly now for McRae as he enjoyed the spring and summer months with Louise, working the farm at Qualicum Beach, and then toiling during the winter as a senator in Ottawa. His lifetime had been crowned with achievements, and he was able to look back on his many accomplishments with a degree of satisfaction. Sadly, his health was beginning to fail and he often had bad days sprinkled in amongst the good ones. Never a man who gave up easily, Senator McRae had worked hard to finish a report for a Senate committee, completing it only a few days before illness forced him into hospital. There were multiple causes of death and he must have known his life was drawing to a close. He died on June 26, 1946.

The next day Senator Gerry McGeer spoke in the Senate of Canada about the death of his colleague and worthy opponent. He rose to offer a tribute to his old foe.

> As a member from British Columbia and one who knew Senator McRae for many years, in fact I lost to him in the 1926 federal election, I would like to add my tribute to that paid by Senator Donnelly. He is a veteran member of the Senate who sat in this chamber with the general for about fifteen years, and is well aware of the great service rendered by this man not only to his city and province but to all of Canada, a country where he had traveled to every corner and knew so well.

Senator McRae died yesterday, one week after he was admitted to hospital. Senator Donnelly said it had been obvious for some time that the general's health was failing and he doubted that the old soldier would make the committee meeting that he was scheduled to attend the day he died. Senator Donnelly pointed out that our colleague was working on a report to be presented at this meeting. He is convinced that only a man of iron will such as Senator McRae could have carried on as he did to finish that report. He did, and then phoned Senator Donnelly to confirm that he would not make the meeting but that the report, his last mission, was ready. Hours later he went to the Ottawa Civic Hospital, and he died yesterday a week later.

Senator Donnelly has pointed to the general's many achievements, particularly his role in helping bring people in to populate the prairies at the turn of the century. He cited the work in his later years at the McRae farm at Eaglecrest on Vancouver Island to improve the quality of crops and livestock. Senator McRae, as Senator Donnelly has pointed out, was a man of strong convictions. When asked why he had brought to Eaglecrest a flock of black-faced sheep from Scotland, the general said simply that he liked them and he was a Scot.

Shortly after he came to Vancouver in 1907 he built a magnificent mansion, Hycroft, on the ridge of Shaughnessy Heights overlooking his city. In 1942 he gave it to the government of Canada for use as a military hospital during the Second World War. I don't think there was any feature of his many successes that he looked on with more pleasure. Nothing pleased him so much as to go there to see to talk and to reminisce with the veterans who were enjoying the delightful surroundings that he was privileged to give them.

He was a driving force with a vigorous constitution and unlimited vision. In his many and various activities he always proudly observed this rule: public affairs were of importance enough to demand and to receive a very substantial portion of both his time and his ability. He was one of the businessmen who realized that the nation's affairs need the guidance of those who have success in private affairs and have demonstrated their ability to serve their country. I knew him in the heat of partisan political fights, and in quieter times, and always recognized that he was a man of conviction.

The *Vancouver Sun* told its readers: "Finis was written to an epoch in development of the West when businessmen and political associates and rivals joined to carry the late Senator Alexander Duncan McRae to his final resting place in the crypt at Ocean View Memorial Park." The *Sun* added that he had a "brilliant financial and political career" and that he "never lost his Midas touch and his ability to read a financial statement was local legend." He was a "tried and true rugged individualist who believed people should stand on their own two feet," the paper stated, recalling that in the 1930s he had campaigned to get Canada out of the League of Nations and free of foreign entanglements.

When McRae died in Ottawa, *Canadian Press* sent out his story across the country, recounting his colourful career. The wire service stated that the senator died of hemorrhaging of the stomach and liver plus a serious blood complaint. It said his colleagues remembered him for his powers of promotion and organization and as a man "willing to take a gamble in ventures of logging, mining and fishing," always ready to take a loss and come back. *Canadian Press* also stated that in later years McRae grew the finest grains and hay on his model farm, Eaglecrest. His hobbies included shooting and fishing, and he was a good horseman.

McRae's death "deprived B.C. of one of the industrial pioneers who made this province what it is today," stated the *Vancouver News Herald.* The senator could have stayed in Minnesota where he had his first success, the paper wrote, "but his considerable talents would have been lost to B.C., to Canada and to the British Commonwealth. He had the vision to foresee the tremendous possibilities of this province."

The *Province* was unable to pay tribute to a Conservative it had supported for many years because it was not publishing due to a labour strike at the paper. The *Victoria Colonist* said B.C. had lost "a sturdy, vigorous fighter," a colourful Canadian who had excelled in the fields of finance and politics.

A newspaper picture in the *Vancouver Sun* showed his flower-covered draped coffin being carried from Canadian Memorial Church, which was filled to capacity for what was described as a "simple impressive ceremony." The old general would have been accorded military honours if the family had requested them, but they decided the service would be simple. Many people stood outside on the sidewalk on Burrard Street to pay their respects to a man that had played a major role in the early days of British Columbia life and had left an industrial legacy. Even those who had been his fiercest political foes extended their respect, as did some of those who saw him in life as a multi-millionaire capitalist and a natural opponent of the working class.

Reverend G. Harrison Villett conducted the brief service. He cited McRae's numerous accomplishments in the very different areas of his busy life. McRae was a man who gave his undivided attention and all his energy, drive, and commitment to the tasks he undertook. Villett spoke of the private man: "I will not deal with the qualities of body and mind which made him one of Canada's best known men. It is the qualities of heart and spirit which make him important, qualities not known to many of his intimate friends." He told the gathering that McRae had talked to him several years previously about the principles he had learned from his family on the farm at Glencoe, when labour was hard, the days were long, and the reward at the end of each was 50 cents. "This was the faith that sustained him and he believed it was the force that brought such a large measure of success to his work," the minister told the mourners.

A soloist rendered the 23rd Psalm, and the congregation sang, "Abide with Me." Accompanying McRae's widow was his daughter, Mrs. Lucile Paul, and his granddaughter, Mrs. Bebe Placker, of Seattle; his youngest daughter Mrs. Margaret "Peggy" Hay Chapman, of Los Angeles, and his other two granddaughters, Jocelyn and Audrey Baker, whose mother Blanche predeceased McRae. Representing the federal government was MP Ian McKenzie, and among the honorary pallbearers were Premier John Hart and McRae's long-time friends Austin Taylor, Vic Spencer, and F.E. Burke.

The flag at Hycroft was flown at half-mast on the day of the funeral, in honour of the man who had built the mansion and then given it to the federal government. Many of the wounded veterans still at Hycroft remembered the general who frequently returned to visit and chat with them. They used flowers from the gardens—blooms that McRae often identified to friends as he strolled the grounds—to make one of the largest wreaths at the church service. A few of the more able veterans came to Canadian Memorial to pay their last respects personally.

In the Abbey at Ocean View cemetery, his plaque on the rose-coloured walls states simply: Senator Alexander Duncan McRae, C.B., 1874-1946. Three other members of his family are nearby, but not in a family grouping as might have been expected. His first wife, Blaunche, is to one side. McRae lies above the body of his eldest daughter, Blanche. Across the aisle lies Lucile, who was 51 when she died in Vancouver on August 29, 1955. She also remarried and returned to Vancouver a few years before she died. Her second husband was Gordon Willard, an interior decorator and owner of the well-known Chelsea Shop, whose clientele were the residents of Shaughnessy. McRae's youngest daughter Peggy lived the longest of the trio and died at the age of 66 in San Francisco on November 21, 1972. She is not entombed with the family at Ocean View.

The End of Eaglecrest

When Alexander McRae died in 1946, the house and acreage at Eaglecrest were almost immediately put up for sale. McRae's wife Louise had lived in the home for only part of the three years they spent together. She had no real attachment to the property and was anxious to return to Texas. McRae's two surviving daughters were both long-time residents of the United States with fewer ties to Eaglecrest than to Hycroft. The property was also so large that few would be interested in maintaining it; although McRae's daughter Peggy could probably have done so if circumstances had been different. She was, however, newly married to Bruce Hay Chapman and living in California. It was inevitable that the 4,000-acre farm would be split off from the waterfront estate. Vancouver lumber baron H. R. MacMillan bought the farm and renamed it Arrowsmith. The real estate firm of Boultbee-Sweet purchased the 260 acres at Qualicum Beach, and initially these two prominent B.C. families continued to use Eaglecrest as a country residence, just as the McRaes had done. It was a wonderful retreat for the owners, Ernest Leonard Boultbee and Frederick Sweet, and their children.

The Boultbees had a long relationship with the McRaes, so it is likely Alexander Duncan would have approved of the new owners. William W. Boultbee, Ernest's brother, was an old friend and a partner of Austin Taylor, one of the original committee of 100 that formed the general's ill-fated Provincial Party. Over the years the various members of the Boultbee family had been guests at Hycroft and Eaglecrest.

John Boultbee, a son of E. L., recently sat in his Vancouver office and recalled the first visit the family made to the new property when it was acquired.

> It was quite astounding. Everything was left as it had been when the family lived there, even the clothes in the cupboards. It was as though they just walked away one day and never returned. There was a fabulous collection of Italian pottery, which the first Mrs. McRae must have brought from Hycroft, and a huge library of books many of them on Alaska and the Canadian north, which we donated to the University of B.C. In McRae's den was a stuffed cougar and there were other wild animal heads on the wall. There was even a 1939 LaSalle touring car up on blocks in the garage. It had obviously been mothballed during the war when there was a shortage of gasoline and there it was in almost perfect condition. When my wife and I married I managed to commandeer it and it was delightful to drive off on our honeymoon in a vehicle like that.

The LaSalle was the vehicle originally purchased by Blaunche McRae so that their governess could drive her grandchildren around the neighbourhood.

John Boultbee described Eaglecrest as a wonderful place with a huge croquet lawn, its own golf course, and those marvelous bridal paths. The McRaes and their guests always dressed for dinner he recalled. One of his father's favourite anecdotes remembered the ambiance at Eaglecrest when the women descended the grand stairs in long gowns to the central lounge. Each guest was served one martini before going in to dinner.

As in McRae's time, well-known dignitaries still found Eaglecrest an attractive place to visit. In 1951 when Princess Elizabeth and the Duke of Edinburgh visited Eaglecrest, the princess commented she would love to stay longer. The orchards, the duck ponds, the tranquil landscape, the magnificent horses, and the wonderful network of bridle paths had charmed her.

By the 1960s, however, the cost of maintaining Eaglecrest was skyrocketing, young children had grown older, and partners Boultbee and Sweet decided to turn the estate into a resort. Unfortunately, the lodge with its beautiful pealed cedar logs did not last long in its new role; it burned to the ground on March 23, 1969. The fire started on the roof near one of the chimneys, and despite the efforts of staff and guests who tried to douse the flames with buckets of water, the lodge burned fiercely until there was nothing left. The fire departments of Qualicum Beach, Parksville, and Coombs-Hillier responded to the fire, but could do little to control it; however, they were able to prevent the fire from spreading to the outbuildings. Almost none of the furnishings were salvaged, although four men were able to rescue one very large, heavy, seventeenth century refectory table.

The lodge at Eaglecrest was gone: the carefully selected cedar logs had become ashes, and the wonderful French country and French Canadian furniture had been reduced to charred sticks. The work of the artisans of Qualicum Beach was no more, and it could never be replaced. As soon as was possible the lodge was rebuilt, using log fabrication that simulated the original style, but it was designed as a resort hotel this time rather than a country home and furnished accordingly. In October 1975 the property was sold again to a group of investors, among them Ernest Leonard Boultbee's son John. This time the property was earmarked for new home development. The hotel and six acres were sold separately in December 1975 to a group of Nanaimo businessmen.

The investors built their subdivision around a golf course while retaining the name Eaglecrest. Mike Dyde, Qualicum College Inn, bought the lodge in June 1976 and turned it into a discotheque dubbed "The Screaming Eagle." Fire had destroyed McRae's original Eaglecrest and the replacement also succumbed to the ravages of flames on July 10, 1981. It was never rebuilt. The Qualicum Beach fire department said the fire was suspicious because it seemed to have ignited simultaneously at both ends of the building. Nothing was ever proven.

Nesbitt on McRae

James K. Nesbitt was a writer and columnist for the *Vancouver Sun* for many years. A Victorian with a great love of his city and province, he was also a keen amateur historian who did much to keep alive the province's past. He wrote about politics and was on first-name terms with many of the movers and shakers in the 1950s and beyond.

A column he wrote on March 27, 1969 probably pointed up how much McRae was the private man, despite the many facets of his career. When Nesbitt wrote, McRae had been dead little more than twenty years. The fire that destroyed Eaglecrest in 1969 had piqued his interest in McRae and his career. Nesbitt wrote that many people had asked him about McRae, saying, "I couldn't answer in any detail, and so I looked up the record and found many facts I had not known before."

He then recited the McRae history, noting the man was a rugged individualist and at the same time friendly and hospitable. Nesbitt concluded, "I am sorry that Eaglecrest is no more, but the loss did give me an opportunity to learn a little of the life of a man who was evidently most remarkable." There was no doubt about that, but politically knowledgeable Nesbitt had to look it all up. It wasn't that he had forgotten; it was just that he never knew because despite all that McRae had done, there was little record of him in the history books.

Not long after this column appeared, Nesbitt wrote a follow-up story because someone had approached him in the legislative corridor and told him that Rae Eddie, the New Democratic Party member for New Westminster, was a nephew of Senator McRae's. Nesbitt immediately sought out Eddie who said, "Yes, my mother was an older sister of the senator. She was Flora McRae, the third daughter in the family and hence my full name—John McRae Eddie."

Nesbitt then made the following observation: "I don't know what the senator would think of nephew Rae, fighting in our legislature for organized labour, more social welfare, reduction of working hours and generally for the betterment of the sweating masses ... The senator would not approve, being a foe of government welfare. He thought labour unions were running the country into ruin. He believed every man should stand on his own two feet and go it alone. However, I think the senator would have been proud that his nephew had the rare glory, back in 1952, of personally defeating a Liberal premier (Byron Johnson)."

Veteran Vancouver lawyer Phil Shier also recalled the love-hate relationship that existed between the socialist-labour union leader and the capitalist uncle to whom he was politically totally opposed. Shier told of a meeting held near Hycroft. When Eddie was late arriving, he apologized, saying that he couldn't resist driving past Hycroft simply to have another look at the "old family home." This was a gentle joke by a man who didn't darken Hycroft's doorway, but obviously felt a tug.

Rae Eddie, like his uncle, was born in Appin, near Glencoe, August 23, 1900, one of four children of John and Flora Eddie. They moved to Saskatchewan in 1903 and then on to B.C. in 1922. Rae joined the union movement in 1944 and was elected to the legislature as the NDP member for New Westminster in 1952. He represented the riding for seventeen years, until he retired at the age of 69. He died in February 1977, aged 76.

Only two of McRae's sisters remained in the Glencoe area: Mary, who was the second oldest girl, and Sara, the sixth, born just before Alexander. Both of them, Mary McRae Oxley and Sara McRae Earle, are buried at Oakland cemetery near Glencoe. One of Sara's daughters, Mrs. Edith Lockwood, remained a Glencoe resident as the new millennium began.

McRae's namesake from the Appin School in Glencoe predeceased him by two years. A. A. McRae, who moved to Minneapolis in 1899 and eventually became chairman of the board of Fourth Northwestern National Bank, died on May 1, 1944 at age 74. He remained a resident of the United States throughout his life and never returned to Canada. The local newspaper's story about his death stated that after a long list of services to Minnesota, the state where he lived most of his life, his family home at 2446 Park Avenue had been sold to the city the previous year and had become the residence of Sister Kenny. Both men named Alexander McRae from Glencoe were extremely successful in business, and both seemed eager to make a final grand donation of property. But even if the slightly older Alexander A. McRae was emulating the younger one, it is doubtful that his gift to the city of Minneapolis was as generous as Alexander D. McRae's gift of Hycroft to the Canadian government.

During his lifetime, the image of the man from Hycroft was written large across the Canadian landscape. His influence on the country, on the settlers, and on the enterprises he developed was significant. There are now but few who remember the man, his exploits, his adventures, or his good works. Nothing remains except Hycroft and the memories of generations of Vancouverites who walked its halls and garden paths, admired the view from the terrace, and partied in its generous salons and the grand ballroom.

McRae's Legacy

The very short McRae Avenue is all there is in today's Vancouver that is named after the farm boy from Glencoe. His grand-daughters moved away, so there are no descendants of Alexander Duncan McRae in Vancouver to keep his name alive in the city by the sea that he chose to make his own.

Only one of his daughters, Blanche, lived in the city after she was married. Her life was short though; she was only 42 when she died. Blanche and her husband Richard Baker had a stormy, often petulant, marriage according to some of their friends, who still shake their heads, saying they had so much and yet the end was tragic. Blanche's second marriage to Daniel Lewis was so short—less than a year—that it hardly counted, especially since she spent most of that time in Tranquille and then in hospital in Victoria until she died.

Blanche's children, Jocelyn and Audrey, were aged 21 and nineteen when she died. Jocelyn had been invalided out of the Wrens with severe back injuries and Audrey was discharged shortly after her mother's death in 1945. The sisters shared an apartment in Vancouver on Cambie Street for about a year, both attending the University of B.C. Jocelyn had been living there under the caring eye of Annie, the family cook from Hycroft, and had began to study commerce and arts before Audrey joined her. Audrey was the first to leave when she took a job as an accountant in Penticton.

Jocelyn later went on to study at the Sorbonne in Paris where she met her husband, Lawrence Patrick Redmond Roche, a lawyer working for the BBC. They were married in St. James Catholic Church, Spanish Place, London. During the nuptial mass she wore an heirloom veil that had belonged to her maternal grandmother, worn at the wedding in 1900 in Minneapolis when a young Alexander Duncan McRae married Blaunche Latimer Howe. Her aunt Lucile McRae Paul gave Jocelyn away. Her aunt Peggy with husband Bruce Hay Chapman of Santa Barbara also attended the wedding. Jocelyn Roche has lived in London England ever since. She has four children—Patrick, David, Christopher, and Anita—all of whom reside in Great Britain.

While Audrey never returned to live in Vancouver, she remained in British Columbia for much of her life. She married Frank Wittner in 1950 and together they were involved in ranching near Kamloops and in the Hidden Valley. Audrey had five children: Frances who lives in Sparwood, Gail who lives in Sicamous, and Richard, Dianne, and Marilyn who all live near Calgary and are the reason Audrey moved to Alberta. She wanted to live near her grandchildren. Audrey had a dream to become a rancher from the days when her grandfather had taken her to the Flying U Ranch in the Caribou, and it was one she was able to fulfil.

Hycroft Is Reborn

McRae's gesture in donating his beloved home as a hospital for ailing veterans of the First and Second World Wars provided Hycroft with a second lease on life. However, this too came to an end on June 2, 1960. As many of the last 60 old soldiers now required more intensive care than the Hycroft Hospital could provide, they were transferred back to Shaughnessy Veterans Hospital some blocks away, and the Hycroft Hospital closed. Maintaining the house and the upkeep of the grounds had become an expensive proposition for the Department of Veterans Affairs, and the deterioration of the property was becoming obvious. The decision made, the federal government put the property up for sale; but, there were no immediate purchasers. One developer wanted to subdivide the land, tear down the mansion, and rebuild. The affluent and powerful residents of Shaughnessy and the city of Vancouver vetoed the proposal.

At age 50 the huge old house sat dark and dilapidated, but still imposing. Green algae began to creep up the white marble stairs of the terrace, and the ten tall north-facing columns were pelted each winter by the blustering wind that swept in from the ocean or down from the mountains laden with rain and occasional snow. Water gushed down the drains, which had become clogged with leaves from the trees, and overflowed. The concrete facade was streaked with rivulets of grime, and leaves cluttered the walkways and lawns, choked the circular drive, filled the mouldering fountain, and piled up behind the gates at 1489 McRae Avenue. It was an eerie place, echoing with ghosts of the past and occasionally visited by curious youths or vandals, especially at Halloween. The lone caretaker E. Kleinsorge and his dog patrolled the grounds, doing their best to discourage unwanted visitors, protecting the dark mausoleum that had once blazed with lights, echoed to high jinx and laughter, and then served the injured of the country as no other building of its kind ever did.

Then one day there were rumours that someone was about to purchase the huge old home. The sale was of considerable interest to any resident who remembered Vancouver in the 1920s, 1930s, or 1940s, because as an irreplaceable Shaughnessy landmark, Hycroft represented more than any other mansion: it was a symbol of an earlier affluence in Vancouver.

The unsuccessful early bid for the property brought the mouldering mansion to the attention of a group of influential Vancouver women whose organization, the University Women's Club of Vancouver, was formed on May 11, 1907, about the time the McRae family moved to the city. For many years, the women had raised, saved, and invested funds in the hope of amassing enough to purchase a clubhouse. In the eight years from 1954 to 1962, their building fund had grown from $17,000 to a tidy $52,000.

At a general meeting that year the club set up a committee of four women to investigate the possibility of purchasing the Hycroft property. Each of them had been involved with raising funds for the project that now might be within their grasp. Hycroft was even more than they had hoped for: a symbol of Vancouver's heritage, an unparalleled landmark, as well as an oasis close to the centre of things in the ever growing city. It was a near perfect location for the club.

Since the federal government had originally acquired Hycroft with an investment of one dollar, the university women decided their first bid on the property—which was now in an advanced state of disrepair—would also be one dollar. It was rejected. The Crown Assets Disposal Corporation made a counter offer to sell the entire estate for $70,500. The sum was beyond the reach of the club. The women continued to be interested, however, and sought alternatives to the outright purchase of the whole five

Today, Hycroft looks much as it did when it was built in 1911. Verdant Virginia creeper climbs the entrance pillars, and the sequoia tree—now 100 feet tall—continues to dominate the garden. Many of the trees McRae brought from around the world continue to enthrall club members and their guests.

and a half acres. Many options were studied before an offer was made to purchase the three western lots, an area of approximately 2.5 acres and about half of the original estate. This portion included the house, stables, and garage as well as half of the extensive walled gardens. The government was insistent that they dispose of the entire property at one time, so negotiations continued; the University Women's Club was given until April 1, 1962 to find an acceptable buyer for the other half of the estate.

Originally pessimistic about their chances, the women persevered and finally found a buyer with a proposal that might be approved by the necessary three levels of government as well as by the residents of the area. An agreement of sale was signed on June 4, and the complicated finalization of the deal began. An order in council approving the sale and conveyance was passed in the provincial legislature on July 3. Letters patent received by the women in late August were returned to the federal government for amendments and received again in mid-November. The next hurdle was an approach to the provincial government to make an amendment to the Shaughnessy Heights Building Restriction Act. It was finally introduced in the legislature, permitting the club to acquire the property, and was proclaimed by the Lieutenant Governor in Council on January 15, 1963.

The purchase price of half the property by the University Women's Club was $30,500. The other half was purchased for a similar amount by a development firm with plans to construct the city's first luxury condominiums. The new owner stated he would retain the recreation building with its swimming pool and indoor sports facilities for the use of the buyers of the luxury units. Shaughnessy residents agreed to the condiminiums, even though it was a radical departure, because it meant preserving Hycroft.

The women's club issued non-interest-bearing debentures in order to cover the costs of restoring the estate. However, as they toiled to restore the mansion to its former glory, they knew the time was drawing near when an instalment payment must be made. To this end, in September 1963, the club sponsored its first Antique Fair in the newly refurbished Hycroft. A huge segment of the city's population turned out to see what had been accomplished. Opened by the lieutenant governor, the fair attracted more than 10,000 people. The finance committee easily made its first repayment to the sinking fund for the debenture issue. A new fund-raising project, the brainchild of Lois Youngson and June Ames, was introduced in November 1973. "Christmas at Hycroft" has since become a favourite family fair for many Vancouver families. Along with weddings, special parties, and Christmas events, there has recently also been a New Year's Eve masquerade ball where a dance band plays the latest songs, the food is delicious, and the house is once again on display. While it's very different from the grand balls of old, Blaunche and Alexander are still very much a part of the scene. Their portraits hang in the lounge where they so often entertained in years gone by.

In 1974, the City of Vancouver declared the property a heritage site to be retained in as near to its original state as possible. This designation is an appropriate reminder of Vancouver's "Days of the Merchant Princes."

More Than A Clubhouse

It had taken the University Women's Club more than a year to complete the ambitious purchase of Hycroft, which by that time had become near and dear to every member of the club, and it would take another year before 100 volunteers were able to repair and furnish their new home. The Interior Development Committee of four included Mrs. Rupert (Alice) Neil, Mrs. Wallace (Miriam) Dorrance, Mrs. O.R. (Violet) Hougen, and Mrs. J. M. (Betty) Mather, whose father-in-law had been one of McRae's Provincial Party Committee of 100.

Their first difficult decision was for the future of the stables. The two-storey structure that adjoined the main house at right angles had been unused since the 1930s when the McRaes built Eaglecrest. It was decided that there was no alternative but to demolish it. Its repair was not possible because the energies of the members along with the club's dwindling funds were fully allocated for the extensive renovations required to refurbish and preserve the house itself. The old mansion was not just run down—nothing was in working order. Repair or replacement was required for the heating system, plumbing, and electrical service. The roof required extensive gutter replacement as well as restoration and cleaning of the green Italian roof tiles. City by-laws required that new fire exits be constructed and that a hard surfaced parking lot be built on the grounds; this requirement then necessitated another difficult decision because it meant the Roman fountain the circular marble pond and rose garden must be sacrificed for it.

Its years as a hospital had wreaked havoc with the old mansion. The linoleum that covered all the floors now needed to be removed so that the oak beneath could be brought back to life through refinishing or replacing. Damaged panelling needed to be repaired and polished. Fireplaces were uncovered and new dampers installed. Even the sprinkler system, installed during Hycroft's years as a hospital, required updating.

Club members, friends and acquaintances were encouraged to donate appropriate furnishings, and in this way three crystal chandeliers, shining table silver, and brass fittings for the fireplaces were gradually acquired. Some nearby residents who had originally purchased furniture at the auction in 1942 now returned it, as

It was difficult for the University Women's Club to duplicate the décor and furnishings from the estates of Europe that had been chosen by Blaunche McRae; however, some neighbours in Shaughnessy returned items they had purchased at the Hycroft auction in 1942, and the women devised various ways to restore some of the panelling to its original condition.

they said, "to where it belongs"; however, much of it required reconditioning, reupholstering, or refinishing.

The University Women's Club organized a volunteer committee to undertake furniture restoration so that it would closely reflect the taste and ambiance once favoured by Alexander and Blaunche McRae. In the first few years after the acquisition of the house, 146 members contributed 1,444 hours of work that was spent cleaning and polishing, sewing and recreating some of the original draperies, sanding the beautiful wooden surfaces, painting, varnishing, and polishing.

A gardening committee retained as much as possible of the original gardens, although many of the flowerbeds were simplified in order to accommodate their care. Today McRae's sequoia (sequoiadendron giganteum) towers 100 feet above the grounds. Sequoia trees that rise from a broad buttress can reach a height of 300 feet in the wild, but seldom rise above 100 feet under cultivation. The copper beech he planted to the east of the house is the largest in western Canada. The yellow flowering davidia trees, which are native to China and were first imported to North America in 1904, still flourish as do many of the other original plantings. The cypress trees along McRae Avenue, however, became diseased and have had to be replaced.

One Man's Remarkable Life

When it was all over, what had the long years meant to Alexander Duncan McRae? Like every other life, his had its share of triumphs and defeats, joys and sorrows. He soared higher than most but also suffered many disappointments. When he might have played a major role in the political life of his country, he was defeated at the polls while the Tory party he had helped rejuvenate won an election and took over the role of government under a man he worked to make its leader. McRae said little publicly about his feelings on these occasions and seldom expressed his inner thoughts. He accepted both victory and defeat without bravado or recrimination, exultation or tears; although, lost opportunity in his two political ventures must have been disappointing to this man of action.

McRae learned early to take chances and was always prepared to pay the price. He was reserved and often reticent to boast about himself, and this trait kept him off the pages of history books about Canada's early settlement and development. His role has consequently been overlooked, and he has become an enigma.

His was the archetypical story of the 50-cents-a-day farm boy who made good, relying on a keen brain and the astute prescience of the entrepreneur to make his millions. It was said that from his earliest business days he could read a balance sheet and envisage a bottom line better than almost anyone. A capitalist who opposed anything resembling a welfare state, he also felt it was the responsibility of government to provide—when necessary—opportunities for employment for individuals truly in need. He was an advocate of massive public works to attain these goals.

McRae knew his limitations. He never had a messianic approach to politics, appreciating before it was recognized by others that his talents were as an organizer and planner rather than as a leader. He readily admitted he was not a backslapping, gregarious "glad-hander," able to work a room or an audience. Still, he was a friendly, likeable man with many friends. While in pursuit of his political goals he mixed in political circles and with members of the media because he felt it necessary, but he did not do this by choice or inclination. Throughout his life he abhorred the loss of economic opportunities that his province or his country failed to utilize as well as the political squandering of public funds. These perceptions were his motivating reasons for creating his Provincial Party in the 1920s when it seemed no one else was prepared to institute the kind of change he felt was essential. It's intriguing to conjecture what B.C. politics might have become if ballot-box stuffing had not robbed him of a win in 1924.

Like the 100 leading Vancouver business and professional men who signed the party manifesto and the majority of the province's people of the time, including the clergy and the blue-collar worker, he feared the "yellow peril" and its perceived threat to jobs, the economy, and the basically British way of life by continued immigration from the Orient. McRae never spoke of better or lesser peoples, or any god-given rights of whites. However, he shared the view of the time that a flood of newcomers of vastly-differing cultures menaced the prevailing lifestyle of early twentieth century British Columbia.

McRae enjoyed the good life and was proud of his mansion— the most obvious symbol to society of his achievements. He was a generous and genial host to his friends and the people of Shaughnessy who attended the glittering functions that Blaunche organized at Hycroft. His wealth was there to be spent and enjoyed; however, he did not lord it over others. He was courteous and generous to his staff, often taking the time to thank them personally for helping to make any event he hosted a success. Wages and working conditions for his staff were good for the times. Similar high standards prevailed at the Fraser River Mill sites when he was actively involved in their operation.

His grandchildren and their friends remember him as a gentle, benevolent man who welcomed them all at Eaglecrest where he spent much of the last decade of his life. They delighted in his teasing and the jokes he told. One granddaughter recalled that he had a wonderful smile and the other commented, "I adored him." McRae had been an indulgent father with his three daughters, and he must have watched their later problems with a sad heart. He was perhaps even more indulgent with his three granddaughters, because by then he had the time to spend with them that he had not been able to give his daughters. As teenagers they were encouraged to invite friends to Eaglecrest, and he provided them with a companion, or a governess, who drove the young people wherever they needed to go and slept with them in the dormitory upstairs at night, being generally responsible for keeping the exuberant youngsters out of trouble.

McRae, the man who made his first millions when income tax was unheard of, was well aware that times had changed when he made his address to the public for the opening of Hycroft as a military hospital. He acknowledged that untrammelled wealth was a thing of the past and correctly prophesied that Vancouver would not see any more estates like his. He had made money and also spent it. He had no regrets.

Although his health was good at the time, his services were not called on in any meaningful way when Canada again entered a world war. McRae had predicted it was coming with chilling accuracy, and at the outset was highly critical of the state of Canada's preparedness. He was well aware—from his earlier knowledge of the needless slaughter in the First World War—of the price to be paid for faltering, amateurish management of a military force. It is difficult to imagine why his organizational and management experience was not called on.

Alexander Duncan McRae threw all his strength and commitment into the challenges and opportunities that confronted him in life. He liked to see things through to the end. In failing health he worked on a Senate committee report, for which he was responsible, until it was finished; then he was admitted to hospital. An era ended when the man from Glencoe died a week later. From prairie land development to west coast fishing, mining, and forestry enterprises, and from provincial and federal politics to experimental farming and stockbreeding on Vancouver Island—he had put his stamp on them. His interests were far-reaching and at times visionary. The development of British Columbia's vast Peace River district is a major economic and social factor in today's world, and the attractions of the Garibaldi region to Whistler Mountain are now internationally recognized; McRae envisioned both many years earlier. He refused, however, to emphasize or exaggerate the role he had played, so it was soon forgotten by most. Nevertheless, tangible results of his accomplishments remain today. They may not be readily identifiable with the man, but they are among the building blocks of his country's early development and economic future. His successes and failures are examples that should be recognized, learned, and not forgotten.

Alexander Duncan McRae, you should have left more of your papers in safe keeping so they could have told your story. We wish we knew you better.

Bibliography

Primary Sources
B.C. Legislative Library, Victoria
B.C. Ministry of Human Resources, Victoria
B.C. Provincial Archives, Victoria
Carnegie Library, Little Falls, Minnesota
Coquitlam Heritage Society
Coquitlam Municipal Library
Duluth Public Library, Duluth, Minnesota
Morrison County Historical Society, Little Falls, Minnesota
National Archives, Ottawa
National Library, Ottawa
Mackin House, Maillardville
Qualicum Historical and Museum Society, Qualicum Beach
Societe Maillardville Uni, Maillardville
Statistics Canada, Ottawa
University Women's Club Archives, Vancouver
Vancouver Archives
Vancouver City Library

Books and Magazines
Canadian Parliamentary Guide, several editions.
Aldred, Robert William. *The Public Career of Major-General Alexander D. McRae*. London, ON: Graduate paper—University of Western Ontario, 1970.
Dafoe, John. *Clifford Sifton in Relation to His Times*. Toronto: Macmillan, 1931.
Davis, Chuck. *Port Coquitlam Where Rails Meet Rivers*. Madeira Park, BC: Harbour Publishing, 2000.
Davis, Chuck. *The Vancouver Book, First Edition*. North Vancouver: J.J. Douglas, 1976.
Dictionary of Canadian Biography, 1910 to 1920. Toronto: University of Toronto Press, 1981.

Ford, Arthur Rutherford. *As The World Wags.* Toronto: Ryerson Press, 1950.

Hamilton, Zachary and Marie. *These Are the Prairies.* Toronto: Toronto School Aids Textbook Publishing, 1948.

Hawkes, John. *The Story of Saskatchewan and its People.* Chicago: Clarke, 1924.

Haycock, Ronald. *Sam Hughes, The Public Career of a Controversial Canadian 1885-1916.* Waterloo: Wilfred Laurier University Press in co-operation with Canadian War Museum, 1986.

Keenleyside, Hugh L. *Memoirs of Hugh L. Keenleyside.* Toronto: McLellan and Stewart, 1981.

Kloppenborg, Anne. *Vancouver's First Century, a City Album, 1860-1960.* Vancouver: J.J. Douglas, 1977.

Kluckner, Michael. *Vanishing Vancouver.* Vancouver: Whitecap Books, 1990.

Locke, Edwin. *The Prime Movers—Traits of the Great Wealth Creators.* New York: AMACOM, 2000.

MacDonald, Bruce. *Vancouver, A Visual History.* Vancouver: Talon Books for Vancouver Historical Society, 1992.

Makowski, L.W. "Rise and Fall of the Merchant Princes." In *Vancouver Magazine.* Vancouver: June, 1911.

McDonald, Robert A.J. *Making Vancouver 1863-1913.* Vancouver: UBC Press, 1966.

Monk, H.A.J. and J. Stewart. *A History of Coquitlam and Fraser Mills.* New Westminster: Jackson, 1958.

Moore, Vincent. *Gladiator of the Courts.* Vancouver: Douglas & McIntyre, 1981.

Morgan, Henry James. *Canadian Men and Women of the Time.* Toronto: William Briggs Publishing, 1912.

Morley, Alan. *Milltown to Metropolis.* Vancouver: Mitchell Press, 1974.

O'Leary, M. Gratton. "The Rival Chiefs of Staff." In *MacLean's Magazine.* Toronto: July 1, 1930.

Paradis, Norah. *The Clan McRae—A Canadian Celidh.* Lantzville, BC: Oolican Books, 1977.

Pare, Andrew. *Fraser River Sawmills 1889 - 2000.* Maillardville: A.G. Pare, 2000.

Pare, Andrew. *The Mansions on the Hill.* Maillardville: A.G. Pare, 1984.

Regehr, T.D. *The Canadian Northern Railway—Pioneer Road of the Northern Prairies, 1895-1918.* Toronto: Macmillan, 1976.

Riou, Jean. *A 75 Year Chronicle of Maillardville, 1909 - 1984.* Maillardville: Society Maillardville-Uni, 1984.

Schreiner, John. *The Refiners: A Century of B.C. Sugar*. Vancouver: Douglas & McIntyre, 1989.

Short, Adam. "Canada and Its Provinces"In *Vol X1X The Prairies*. Edinburgh: Edinburgh University Press, 1914.

Stewart, John. "Early Days at Fraser Mills 1889-1912." In *Lumber B.C. Magazine*.

Van Brunt, Walter. *Duluth and St. Louis County, Their Story and People*. Chicago and New York: The American Historical Society, 1921.

Walker, Russell. *Politicians of a Pioneer Province*. Vancouver: Mitchell Press, 1969.

Watkins, Ernest. *R.B. Bennett, A Biography*. London, ON: Secker, 1963.

Williams, David Ricardo. *Mayor Gerry*. Vancouver: Douglas & McIntyre, 1986.

Yee, Paul. *Saltwater City, An Illustrated History of the Chinese in Vancouver*. Vancouver: Douglas & McIntyre, 1988.

Newspapers:
Canadian Press
The Globe, Toronto
The Leader, Regina
Little Falls Daily Transcript, Minnesota
Little Falls Herald, Minnesota
New Westminster Columbian
The Northwest Magazine, Minnesota
Searchlight
Vancouver News Herald
Vancouver Province (formerly *Vancouver Daily Province*)
Vancouver Sun
Victoria Daily Colonist
Victoria Times
Winnipeg Free Press

The majority of the photographs for this book were provided by the University Women's Club. Others came from the granddaughters of Alexander Duncan McRae and the authors.

Index

Betty O'Keefe was a *Vancouver Province* reporter for seven years in the 1950s. She worked in corporate communications for fifteen years and was commissioned to write two corporate biographies.

After stints at the *Victoria Colonist* and the *Vancouver Province,* Ian Macdonald joined the *Vancouver Sun* and was legislative reporter in Victoria for five years and then bureau chief in Ottawa from 1965 to 1970. He worked in media relations for the prime minister's office and was head of Transport Canada Information. He has written for magazines, radio, television, and film.

Since 1994 Macdonald and O'Keefe have collaborated on writing projects related to West Coast history. Published books include *The Klondike's 'Dear Little Nugget'* for Horsdal & Schubart through to 1999's best-seller *The Sommers Scandal.* *The Mulligan Affair: Top Cop on the Take,* their first book published by Heritage House in 1997, was nominated for the City of Vancouver Book Award. *The Final Voyage of the Princess Sophia* followed in 1998 and *Canadian Holy War* in 2000.